<u>Changing of Seasons</u>

Written by: Stephan Ray Swimmer

Wordclay
1663 Liberty Drive, Suite 200
Bloomington, IN 47403
www.wordclay.com

First published by Wordclay on 5/22/2008.

ISBN: 978-1-6048-1155-1 (sc)

Library of Congress Control Number: 2008929151

Printed in the United States of America.

This book is printed on acid-free paper.

Preface

Hi, my name is Stephan Swimmer. I am a Native American Indian of the Eastern Band of Cherokee and Chippewa tribes. I was born and raised in the heart of the Great Smokey Mountains of western North Carolina. Where I graduated from High school and received an athletic scholarship to run cross country and track in Lawrence, Kansas at the Haskell Indian Junior College. This is where I got into the Army National Guard then I moved to Arizona to attend Arizona State University. I dropped out after two semesters and went into active duty in the Marines. After ending my enlistment in the United States Marine Corps in 1991, I got a position with Bureau of Indian Affairs (BIA) in the Fire Management seasonal program as a Fire Tower Lookout for one summer in New Mexico. This led to an Engine-crewmember position, lasting several more summer seasons until I got accepted into the Redmond Smoke Jumper program in Oregon. I continued doing this until I suffered injuries from a bad jump that sent me into rehabilitation for several months. After that I made a return to fire by working with helicopters at the Grand Canyon National Park Service Helitack-base in Arizona, until a new position was offered to me with the Black Mesa Hotshots - a Bureau of Indian Affairs type-I training crew in New Mexico. After one season, I decided to move on into a permanent Assistant Fire Management Officer (AFMO) trainee position with the U. S. Forest Service in Mt. View Arkansas. There I got detailed with the Asheville Hotshots in North Carolina which led to my attending the Southwest Fire Use Training Academy in New Mexico. In May 2004, I was offered a new post as Zone AFMO on the Poteau/Cold Springs Ranger Districts in Arkansas. There I was afforded the opportunity to attend the Technical Fire Management program in Washington State. After completing that training I moved back home to Cherokee NC to accept the position as Wildland Fire Prevention Officer for the BIA Eastern Cherokee Agency. Until the smoke jumping accident I worked in fire only during the summer months. During the winter months I had to work many other odd jobs such as a waiter, house construction wood framer, Casino security officer, furniture mover, VA file clerk, native dance performer, I also took more college courses. It was during this time I got into acting and lived in LA for a while but that's another story.

I would like to thank everyone that crossed my path in this life, their shared experiences helped shape this book. This project has truly been a therapeutic spiritual journey for me in which I focus the attention on the positive aspects of my life experiences and will leave the negative in its place somewhere in the past. That's another story. Most importantly, this could not have been completed without the help and encouragement of my wife, friend, editor, and partner in crime. Enjoy.

Stephan Swimmer

Table of Contents

Changing of seasons
Introduction

It's a clear, sunny Sunday afternoon, temperatures in the mid 80's, as an elderly couple drives through a park and passes underneath a banner that reads, "35-Year Retirement Party". The park is like most other city parks that might be seen in downtown urban America. A newly painted, custom 1943 Ford pickup pulls up in front of a large gathering of interracial bystanders. The truck couldn't have attracted more attention if it had been a stretch limo pulling up in front of the red carpet of the Oscar's night in L.A. Like paparazzi attacking famous celebrities, the elderly couple is graciously ushered out of the glossy painted purple custom pickup and escorted to a pavilion that has been decorated with bright color streamers marked for the occasion. Tables lined the interior of the pavilion with a small stage at the far end. Heavy white smoke rises up into the blue sky at the opposite end releasing the tantalizing aroma of a cookout. Children run rampant playing their own games in the luscious green grass which carpets the landscape park. Tall hardwood trees provide ample shade for the event. A gentle breeze blows through the tree branches mixing nature's harmony with the other busy park noises. Squirrels can be seen gathering up food for the coming winter. Dogs are leaping around in circles staying close to their unduly masters as if the green grass is on fire.

As the party gets into full swing, a man stands and

proudly steps-up to the podium at center stage and waves his arms in the air in an attempt to get everyone's attention. As the chaotic chatter subsides enough to be heard, the speaker introduces the retiree. John-John Wilton is asked to speak to the crowd. On this day he is doing exactly what his best friend would have wanted him to do; give something back; leave something positive for future generations to model; share some personal insight of what experience has taught him through all these years and hope through it all someone else could fine solis in the strength of family.

Mr. John-John Wilton is a quiet man despite his massive stature, having a weathered face showing evidences of many years in the sun. He is dressed in a white dress shirt, mixed match suit jacket and wearing black slacks with cowboy boots. He looks at his lovely wife, Sara, sitting obediently beside him in her western style dark brown dress decorated with a full turquoise and silver necklace. She gives him a nod of approval. Slowly, he pushes his chair away from the table and hesitates just long enough to get the crowd cheering and chanting, "Speech! Speech! Speech! As bystanders scramble to help him to the podium, he waves everyone off as if silently saying, "I can do it on my own." Gripping both sides of the podium, he becomes speechless for a moment as he scans the anxious audience. Remembering…

Part 1
All Things Connected

This is how it was told to me a long time ago. The old ones in Cherokee tell us of a spring time long ago when all living things, man, animals and plants could talk to one another. Together, they lived at peace and had a great friendship. As time passed, the population of man grew so much that their disregard to the environment spread across the entire land. The animals, plants and birds soon found their habitats being taken over. To make things worse, man was given the gift of fire, invented tools and then learned to produce lethal weapons with this fire. These humans began to hunt and kill the animals, birds and fish for mere profit. The plants were burned to benefit mans progress alone. The smaller creatures, like the ant, frog and worm were stepped upon and crushed without thought, out of carelessness, and sometimes, even contempt.

The animals decided to hold a council to discuss measures for their safety. The deer decided they would send arthritis to every hunter who killed one of them, unless he made sure to ask forgiveness for the offense. They sent notice of their decision to the nearest settlement of Cherokee and told them how they could avoid this. Now, whenever a hunter shoots a deer, Little Deer, who is swift as the wind and cannot be harmed, goes quickly to the spot and asks the spirit of the deer if it has heard the prayer of the hunter, asking for pardon. If the spirit replies yes, everything is in balance. If the reply is no, Little Deer follows the trail of the hunter to his home. Little Deer enters invisibly and strikes the hunter with arthritis while the hunter is resting. No hunter who regards his own health ever fails to ask pardon of the deer for killing it.

Next, the fish and reptiles held their own council. They decided to make the offender dream of snakes slithering about them, blowing foul breath in their faces. The victim would also smell the stench of decaying fish so they would vomit and lose their appetites if a prayer wasn't said thanking for the food.

Finally the birds, insects and smaller animals assembled for their council. One after another, they complained about man's cruelty and disrespect. The ant spoke up saying something must be done to slow this man's selfish intrusions! Otherwise, the ant feared deprivation to his way of life. The ant said this man is always stomping down a lifetime of achievement and hard work just simply to satisfy his own greed. Next, the birds condemned this man because they scorch their feathers with careless fire and endanger their young. Others followed with their own complaints. The ground squirrel was the only one to say something in this man's defense because he was so small he did not endure the hurting and disrespect. The others became so angry with him they swooped down on him and shredded his fur with their claws. Thus, the stripes on his back can be seen to this day.

The Plants eventually became fond of this man, especially his use of fire to burn off fields to plant crops this kept him out of the wildlands. After hearing about all these things the animals were doing to the people, each tree, shrub and herb agreed to furnish a cure for some of the afflictions. Each said they would appear and help some men if and when they called upon them in prayer. This is how the Cherokee medicines came to be. Every plant has a use, if only we would listen, learn and respect it. They have furnished remedies to counteract diseases brought on by the revengeful animals. One has to learn to listen. Listen to everything that is around you. It will teach you the right way. It will teach you the secrets of when or what season to pick and utilize its remedy. Some are meant for use in the winter, others in the summer, and some in the spring or fall. Everything has a season, even you and I. This is the story that was told to my family a long time ago by Ah-yu-win-ni (Old man Swimmer) the great Cherokee storyteller.

Planting Corn

Summer time could always be reflected on as a warm, happy, fun-filled moment in time in the heart of the Great Smoky Mountains of western North Carolina. Memories of the never ending evergreen landscape, rolling mountains, crystal clear, ice-cold rivers created delight, especially for a young toddler's mind feeding on experience and adventure of every kind.

That was the realm of reality for this skinny kid. It was the primary driving force of existence for a Native American boy named "Obadi".

Considered shy, a loner, and the second youngest of nine siblings, Obadi was forever finding himself in the middle of a fine mess of trouble. Most of the time it wasn't his fault, rather, just the mere fact of being caught in the wrong place at the wrong time. Of course, having the buck passed down didn't help matters. Add all this up and you find someone thriving on trouble merely because he knows he will be blamed for any wrong doing directed at the family anyway.

Obadi accepted his reputation and, as bad as it may sound, the acceptance brought him happiness and peace of mind. He reasoned great strength could be drawn from a strong heart and mind. In fact, his sense of belonging stemmed from these feelings. Every wrong doing seemed justified, even if it was only to himself.

For Obadi the summer was starting innocent enough. Little did he know this would be the endowment of his life's story.

At 9 a.m., on a sunny Monday morning, not a soul was stirring in the household of Obadi. Not even him! Not until Grandpa McGillis came storming in like the Old World War II ex-marine that he was. At the top of his voice he yelled, "Get up and out of bed you bunch of no good, lazy little girls." The shrill command sent everyone scrambling for cover, looking for a place to hide. Grandpa would pour some cold coffee and make himself at home at the kitchen table yelling, "Hurry up, we have work to do".

Where were the parents when all this was going on? The answer is obvious within most working class families in America during the 1970's. Both parents were working of course, to feed the family. In Native American cultures the grandparents take great pleasure in the upbringing and teachings of their children's kids. We all just thought Grandpa McGillis had no one else to pester since Grandma McGillis died two years earlier. Little did we know that he was just trying to show us how hard life was outside of the family or without family. Life wasn't going to be without scarifies and it meant making choices.

All the kids would be hiding in the back, behind one of the bedroom doors, keeping a watchful eye on grandpa. They were whispering to one another, "You go."
"No you go. He likes you."
"No he doesn't, he doesn't like anyone."

They were trying to decide who would be the first to go out and greet Grandpa, buying everyone else some more time. Well, this would go on until everyone looked at little Obadi. With a pause and a lot of reluctance, he had no choice but to go and talk to grandpa. "Good morning gramps, you want more coffee?" Grandpa McGillis would sternly glance over his black-rimmed glasses and huff. That was

Obadi's cue to hurry up and get dressed for work.

Once everyone was up and dressed, Grandpa McGillis would tell us what chores he had in store for us that day. More often than not, the chores consisted of planting and hoeing corn, or weeding the entire garden. On this day, it would be planting corn and everything associated with that. No one would guess these skills would play an important role in developing little Obadi's career path later in life.

One positive benefit to being first was being able to choose which task you wanted before anyone else. In planting logistics, it's easier to drop corn into a hole that someone else has dug, rather than dig the hole yourself. So obviously, this is the one job everyone desires. Today, it would be Obadis'!

Grandpa McGillis always had a certain way of doing things, anything and everything - his way. With this task he would get a bed sheet or pillowcase, tie it over one shoulder and under the other arm. This would create a pouch to carry a lot of corn kernels. The makeshift hopper looked funny, but it was quite efficient. One arm could reach in to scoop up a hand full of corn. The other was free to drop two or three kernels into a hole. Someone in front walks along to dig the planting holes. Another person would follow, covering up the holes. Although the method was fast and effective, a sack of corn seemed to go a long way. As the day wore on, the sun got hotter. In the south, that meant 98% humidity and temperatures in the high 90's. Obadi and the other kids had one thing on their minds, jumping into that ice-cold river at the other end of the field. As they worked, dust-covered sweat dripped into their eyes. The sound of cool, flowing water broke any concentration on the job at hand. All thoughts were focused on the water. Making you lust to be right in the middle of that cool refreshing water.

Grandpa McGillis was way at the other end of the cornfield plowing with the horse. Yes, we were probably the only people still using a horse and plow. Anyway, there was no way he could watch our every move. So, by the time Obadi made his way to the end of one row, dropping two or three kernels of corn seemed foolish. A couple of handfuls seemed more within reason. After about ten long rows, Obadi's job was complete and grandpa thought that was about right, freeing him to go swim first. This too, would come back to haunt Obadi. When the corn started growing, there was always one spot at the end of the rows where a massive amount of kernels would be sprouting up. It was obvious where a lot of corn kernels had been dropped. But Obadi was not alone. Even the old horse figured out a way to beat the sun. Since it was so hot, Grandpa McGillis would let the horse have some water from a bucket placed at one end of the field. The horse started taking longer and longer breaks with his head in the water bucket, or so it appeared. As Obadi walked by the horse, he saw that the animal wasn't even drinking water but sleeping with his head in the bucket. Poor beast! All in the name of corn! The events of the day would dominate discussion at the supper table for years to come. Even when Obadi would come back home and visit family later in life, someone would always bring up the old corn-planting story.

The Swimming Hole

Being raised on the reservation is like being in a world within itself. Glimpses of the outside world were gained through television, but the luxury of television was not available to everyone on the reservation, or even having access to one. Fortunately for us, watching it wasn't as big of a necessity as playing or exploring our own domain. When the two worlds meet, it's purely inquisitive, like satisfying the curiosity. In one sense, Obadi's family was more fortunate than most because they had not one, but two black and white televisions. However, only one had a picture and the other sat on top and had to be turned on in order to get sound. Hey, this is the Reservation I am talking about - a third world country right in the backyard of America, more like a country ghetto.

One mile down the road from Obadi's house was a KOA campground. Fishing was big business on this reservation or "Rez" as we called it. To us Indian kids, this meant easy money. Half the time, tourists at these camps didn't have the patience to look for the perfect hole or even catch a fish. We could sell them a bucket of fish for ten to twenty bucks. That's a lot of money to "rez" kids.

To reach the favorite swimming hole, Obadi and the

16

gang had to follow a small path through a cow pasture with grass as tall as the kids. The pasture also produced a huge apple tree full of treats just ripe for the picking on the return trek home. To navigate the other end of the pasture required speed and agility. It was home to one mean, snorting, puffing black Brahma bull contained by a taut five-strand barbed-wire fence. The fence was too high to climb and strung too small to go through. The kids knew just the right spot where a stump stood next to the fence. At the right speed, one could hop from the top of the stump in one stride, leaping clear over the fence leaving in their dust a black mass of terror that would stomp back and forth attracting the attention of barking dogs. At this point, our route intersected another path well traveled by fishermen along the riverbank. The path contained all kinds of hiding places for the many make-believe war games we liked to play. The route proceeded down around the campground to an enormous single rock at the very edge of the water. The boulder protruded half way across the river making a deep, natural dam. We felt it was placed there just for our enjoyment, and of course everyone else who lived near or just happened upon it. Being on the "rez", this meant mainly cousins or an occasional camper. In the event the swimming hole was occupied, when Obadi and friends arrived, they soon managed to clear it out. Not many folks could relax with a bunch of wild, half-naked (or naked), noisy Indian kids jumping, yelling and splashing in the cool, clear mountain stream. There were rocks and trees to jump from as well as the old tire swing. The water was so cold when you first got in. It was common knowledge around these mountain parts, that if you tried to get in one foot at a time, you would never succeed. The trick was not to think about it and jump right in like the dogs do. Of course, you would jump in feet first due to danger from rocks and logs beneath the surface. The fun would continue until Mom or someone else noticed our lips turning purple. That meant we all had better get out before the whole body pruned.

No one was in a hurry to get home to do more chores today. Everyone always had this instinctive feeling when supper would be ready. Now was playtime, maybe a war game, especially after hearing about it on the television. While everyone was lying around deciding what team to be on and where the boundary lines, if any, would be placed, Obadi was looking in the direction of the campground. With a cold expression on his face, whirling a stem of grass in his mouth, he was making plans of his own.

Campers have a tendency to leave their camps and all their belongings unsecured while they go on their merry way to fish. They would dress in the flashy new fluorescent style outfits one sees in those "Fish and Stream" magazines at the local five-and-dime stores in town. The fancy clothes didn't seem to help catch any fish, because they would end up paying top dollar for some of our fish at the end of the day.

For any native kid that doesn't see the big town but on special occasions, the prospects of what might be in those coolers can be quiet attractive. For Obadi, all his thoughts were focused on one thing - how to get away with this stunt, kind of like a warrior's greed, he thought.

This is how the war game was played. After everyone had divided up into teams, the first team got a head start. The second team laid in wait before taking off after the first. The objective was for the second team to make it to a predetermined destination, which for today was the stump by the fence. The second team would try to make the destination without being taken prisoner by the first team. Obadi was on the second team. As he waited, he continued scheming.

When it was time for the second team to take off, it was determined that the best strategy would be to split up and meet in intervals. That strategy would stay in effect until team two could see the fence, find a counter ambush site, or scope out a emeny sniper at which time he could take out the enemy sniper, then make a unified dash to the stump.

As the second team disbanded in several different directions, Obadi went his own way. It just happened to be a beeline to an abandoned campsite. The campsite had a small, round, tin camper trailer with a picnic table in front of the doorway. A large green tarp was strung out over the top providing nice shade. The tarp seemed unnecessary to Obadi since the camp was already nestled under a thick canopy of trees. Lawn chairs circled a fire pit in front of the table and several coolers lined the background along with other camping gear. Like an eagle swooping down on his prey, Obadi raced through the campsite in one swipe trying to snatch the cooler off the picnic table in full stride. To his surprise, the cooler was heavier than he had anticipated. He was flipped completely around upside down landing flat on his back. It was like trying to pick up a bail of hay soaked with rainwater. The young warrior found himself looking straight up into the beautiful blue sky with the breath knocked from him, listening to his own heartbeat, wishing he could just die. He did not know it could feel even worse.

All of a sudden, a faint voice brought life and unbelievable strength back into Obadi. Determined not to let his efforts go to waste, Obadi sprang to his feet, scooped up the full cooler with much effort and disappeared into the brush.

Stealing from a white man was risky business and we all knew someone would have to pay if caught. But, Obadi also knew that they would have to catch him on his own turf. And, all the skins knew, no white man would venture too far off the trail into the dark forest alone with a bunch of wild savages running free. As the voice got closer, Obadi realized he couldn't lug a full cooler at a very fast pace without frequent rest. That meant, "capture."

For Native Americans, stories are always being passed down of brave deeds warriors/leaders like Crazy Horse, Sitting Bull, Black Elk and others did as kids to help their tribe survive. This was in Obadi's

20

mind as he pondered what to do. The solution was simple. Obadi had to empty the contents out, take only what he could carry and dump the empty cooler into the river. The current would carry the rest of the evidence downriver. Then, he could high tail it back to warn everyone else to get home.

Of course, it wasn't that simple because by now, the campers were searching up and down the river trail. Obadi was cut off between the trail and the river. So Obadi chooses to jump into the river trying to hide. Half his body was shivering in the cold water. The other half was lying miserably under an outcrop of tree roots along the riverbank. Never mind the possibility of poisonous snakes. Obadi could hear conversations going on above his hiding spot. Someone had found the empty cooler floating down the river and mentioned going back to camp to wait for the BIA (Bureau of Indian Affairs) police. Obadi had stashed as many treats as he could into his shirt and tucked the shirt into his pants.

Now it was time to worry because BIA police were local guys. Most of them had grown up with Obadi's dad and knew the area well (one was his uncle). Plus, these guys were not afraid to scout out trouble. However, these same officers are notorious not to be in the best of physical condition. Obadi's dad had stories of his bootlegging days and out running these police on the back roads, but that's another story.

With everyone dispersed, and one of the campers still searching the trail, there was no way of letting the other kids know what was happening. Besides, the less they knew, the better off they would be. Obadi had to get out of this without getting hung.

There were a couple of hard choices to be made. One, he could turn himself in, but justice would surely be one-sided. Today, it sure wouldn't be on his side. He could remain where he was until nightfall. But then, everyone in his family would be out looking for him, eventually having to call the police. No, there seemed to be only one true way out of this situation. That's what he did.

Obadi eased himself into the swift, cold river and began slowly making his way over to the other side. There, he found a bush that would conceal his movement enough to get out and climb the embankment onto an old logging road. It was a long way around, about a mile just to reach the bridge crossing. It was another mile back to the house. Needless to say, Obadi ran the whole way, safely. Safe!

Meanwhile, all the other kids were still playing the war game with no idea of the happenings down stream. By now, the BIA police had graciously shown up to help out with the investigation. On instinct, one officer started upstream on the trail to see if he could find any evidence to the campers claim.

Just about the time the officer was ready to turn around. He heard a noise to the left of the trail.

Stopping, he quickly put his right hand on the revolver. Straining to catch any sound, he turned ever so slowly and with his left hand, pushed aside a branch in the deep, dark thicket. Suddenly, with a thunderous roar and screams of all decimals, rocks, sticks and dirt balls start flying at the BIA officer from the trees on all sides. He didn't have time to react in any way but to ball up and try to fend off as much as possible.

It took a few moments before the first team of kids fully realized exactly who had the misfortune of walking into their perfectly executed ambush. Everyone froze with mouths open wide as if to say, "Oh my God!"

The officer, trying to regain his composure, slowly stood up and looked directly into the trees. Clearing his throat and viciously rubbing his whole body, he said, "Get your butts down here, now!"

He got everyone to stand in a line and what a lineup it was! Half of them had weeds sticking out of their shirtsleeves and branches hanging out of their pants. Others had mud all over their faces.

The officer asked each of them some questions and concluded this bunch couldn't be the ones in the wrong. Heck, they were too much into their game. He just chased them home.

The second team was still hiding in some trees. Waiting for their last member to show up, they had a birds-eye view of what had just transpired. Dying of laughter, they soon joined in on the run across the pasture. Without stopping for their daily treats, they hit the front door of their house and found Obadi lying on the floor amidst an assortment of pop and candy.

Boy Scout Camp

Boy Scouts always seem easy for native kids. Non-natives are always intrigued with learning how to do things we, as natives, already knew as part of our natural upbringing. But, it was fun at any rate because we got to go to all these neat places, which we would have otherwise never seen.

The Boy Scout troop that Obadi belonged to was comprised of boys from the public school he attended. In fact, our fearless leader was the principal Mister Riggs, an ex-Army Ranger who never missed a chance at an attempt to instill military discipline into his scouts.

One of those special moments in scouts is the opportunity to go to the annual summer Boy Scout Camp. It is a two-week camp where one can earn all sorts of merit badges to achieve ranking towards the prestigious Eagle Scout. For reservation boys, it was enticing just to get away and explore. No one ever stuck with it long enough to get as far as Eagle Scout, but skills gained from these experiences could help in later endeavors. Obadi would attest to this later in life.

Only seven of the original twelve could afford to go to camp this summer. John-John, a rich wannabe (someone wanting to be a Indian) who had all the newest and latest camping gear, was so eager and gullible it was pitiful. A classmate and good friend of Obadi, his family owned several gift shops in town. Actually, all he wanted was to fit in with everyone. Mike a tough half-breed, one of Obadi's best friends, was a jokester, loud and boisterous. Vince, a full-breed short for his age, but a snake, was the smallest of the bunch and the sharpest. Paul, a white boy preacher's son, was a hard working farm boy. Camp was a big treat for him. This would be his last adventure with the group. Little Ed, Obadi's foster brother, was a fat kid who had to wear these big government issued black-frame coke-bottle looking glasses. He always seemed to have tape wrapped around one side of the glasses, and the lenses were scratched. You wondered if he could see at all. Little Ed was a couple of years younger than Obadi and worshipped his every move. Obadi always took care of him, good and bad. Last was Big Ed, Obadis' older brother by about four years. He even acted older and didn't have much to do with the younger scouts. He was always doing his own thing and hanging out with the scout masters, truly the good son. In fact this year he would be completing his Eagle Scout requirements. He was the real leader but he stayed out of the way and let Obadi run his buddies around. He never would say it, but one could tell Big Ed held a unique admiration for Obadi and protected him in more ways than one.

Whenever Obadi was in deep trouble, poor innocent Little Ed was right there too, getting punished alongside Obadi. One particular time, Obadi got mad at his parents and talked Little Ed into running away from home with him. The pair made it to downtown, about 7 miles away, before some relatives picked them up on the road trying to hitch a ride. These two little boys were wandering around with no direction or clue to what may lay ahead. Their mom was so frightened. Talk about a whipping - they both got it! Little Ed would say days later that he didn't mind the spanking. He was glad to get picked up because he was getting hungry.

Nicknames are an attribute to which most indigenous people can relate. For Obadi's gang, this was a lingering trait left over from their parent's boarding school days. Native language and/or Indian names were not allowed, so other names came about closely resembling the Indian method of naming individuals. The norm was to choose something like an animal name that strongly represented that individual's spirit. The scouts try to mimic this but to hear non-natives saying a nickname just doesn't sound right. Some are even quite hilarious! One joke Rednecks like to tell among themselves goes something like this; One day an Injun was ask by a cowboy passing by. "Hey chief, got a question for you. How do you all come up with all those funny Injun names?" The chief replies "Ah know how Injuns name their kids?" The cowboy has to answer "No! That's why I ask, Chief." The big

Injun chief slowly looks up in the sky and raises both arm in the air before beginning to speak saying "Ah, a great medicine man goes out side the teepee on the day of birth and the first thing he sees becomes the young ones name. Like Morning dove, dragging canoe, or rain." Than the cowboy says out loud "hot damn so that's how you got your name two dogs screwing." Ha. Ha. Are you laughing?

John-John was known, as "Snake" because of the way he always seemed to know how to get out of work. Mike was "Hawk", something he picked up by his hook nose looks. Vince went by "Mouse" as a result of his big ears and small face. Paul was big and as slow as a "June Bug," a name that followed him onto the football field. Little Ed was "Bear" since the day he showed up everywhere with his faithful teddy bear. Obadi was called "Dawg," "Big Dawg," "Hey Dawg," something he picked up from his uncle who was a former Marine. "Devil Dog" was something his uncle was always yelling at one of his Marine buddies thus something Obadi called everyone else.

Sunday was setup day for all the boys arriving in Boy Scout camp. It wasn't the regular routine of Sunday school, sitting between your parents listening to the stories of this fellow named Jesus from across the ocean and trying to visualize what God looks like. For Native Americans there is another religion, which deals with the elements on this land and the spirits all around us. Our church is nature, but many years of abuse have shunned away those practices.

The parents usually drop off their kids at one of the meeting halls. In our case, it was the local schoolhouse, an old stone building, which would close down after Obadi graduated 8th grade, still a few years away. The stone schoolhouse stood tall on a hill with a large graveled parking area in front flanked by two open fields, used as playgrounds.

On the last day of school everyone said their goodbyes even if camp was only a few weeks away. It was a time of joy. Everyone raced toward the lined yellow school buses. Summer was finally here.

However, time seem to drag by before that week of Boy Scout camp arrived. Finally, the day was at hand. Everyone started eagerly showing up at the school house to go.

Obadi's dad helped out on occasion. This year he volunteered to help drive to camp. This meant embarrassment for the kids. Who wanted to be seen in a green monster, the family car? It was a 1973 Ford station wagon, no hubcaps, maybe two good tires, the paint fading to blend with the color of dirt. The green monster never got washed unless it rained. One side was scratched up and dented, scars from Obadi's dad's moonshine running days but that's another story. No one really wanted to ride in it until faced with the other option, a Volkswagen van piloted by scoutmaster/principal Mr. Riggs. The camp gear was piled in the VW van and on top of the old station wagon. Instead everyone was fighting for the back seats of the station wagon. Kids always seem to like that very back pop up seat in the old station wagon. No one knew at that time, this would be a time to be recounted for years to come.

It was about a three-hour drive up through the mountains of western North Carolina. Everything was flourishing to its fullest color. Green dominated the landscape and the tree canopy shielded out the sweltering southern heat, creating dark shadows between the trees.

With all the windows rolled down, talking was done at the highest volume. Everyone could tell that it wasn't one of Obadi's father's favorite endeavors but he kept it all to himself. He drove on listening to gospel music on the radio, watching the curvy, wondrous road.

Finally, the car turned onto a gravel road and after a distance, total dust-out. Windows were rolled up only to feel the humidity. In unison, the windows were rolled back down. Farther on, a body of water started opening up the canopy of trees - Lake Cherokee. In front of us was the sign reading, "Welcome to Boy Scouts of America." Here it was: Camp.

Camp was nestled by a man-made lake isolated twenty miles away from the nearest town in the heart of the Appalachian Mountains. It had all the modern facilities, like the dining building and cantina right by the lake with all the sleeping quarters arranged in groups along the mountainsides. The lake itself was laid out with a swimming area marked at one end. Canoes were spread out in neat rows at the other end. A giant billboard stood in front of the lake as another welcoming sign and marked the entrance road running along the left side of the lake. A huge spillway extended to the right ending somewhere in the mountains, hidden by the trees.

As everyone unloaded, Obadi's father and Mr. Riggs walked up to the check-in building. It was an old log cabin where other scoutmasters mingled around all dressed up in scout clothes. They were talking about all the upcoming events, greeting each other and discussing the last camp together. There's something about scouts, everyone seems to really accept Native Americans. This was no exception as everyone cleared out of the doorway and ushered in the new arrivals. As Obadi looked at the schedule of events posted on a bulletin board, his eyes got bigger and bigger. There will be canoeing, wilderness survival, archery, swim qualifications, woodcrafts, basketry, pottery and Indian lore. There would be more, hell fire this was going to be everything these boys mastered back on the reservation!

After checking in, the boys were shown on a map just exactly where they would be staying, the very far end of the camp. By the looks of it, it was a long way away from the cafeteria. By the appearance of the place, this camp had it all. A stream fed into the lake on one side and a gravel road followed it up slope to the campsites. Large grassy fields lined both sides.

Huge pine trees shaded the edges. The tents where two-man white army tents erected on wooden platforms, surrounding a rock fire pit in groups of about five tents per campsite.

As everyone buddied-up into twos, each picked a tent in the group that would be home for the week. Obadi chose Mike, which is ironic, considering both were the leaders and instigators of the whole pack. Little Ed and Vincent paired up since they were the same age and they were friends. Paul and John-John didn't really have a choice, but fit nicely.

After everyone got settled down and unpacked, there was time to kill before supper. The principal had to take John-John down to the camp doctor with some kind of special papers, so they said. That's when Obadi and the gang found out about John-John's wealth of goods, a nice silk goose down sleeping bag, a Coleman lantern, snakebite kit and cooking utensils. Things that made this whole Boy Scout idea seem non-essential. The discovery would open the door for the mischievousness that would follow.

It all began as a single act and ended with an all out series of events that could be described as nothing but chaos. Obadi started by planning a scheme; the capture of a garden snake. The mountains were full of them and he wanted to donate one to John-John as a sleeping partner. This act would show John-John that money wouldn't be enough to buy his way into the approval of this tribe. There was something about rich folks these boys hated. Possibly, because they knew that particular materialistic life style was something far from the grasp of their own reality.

However, something bigger started in motion as everyone interpreted his or her own justice here. Vincent went into Obadi and Mike's tent to tell them the mission was completed, the snake, that is.

Paul, who must had been caught up in the excitement, went racing into his own tent and hurled a tent peg through the tent, his own tent! He then crashed the Coleman lantern, startling and bringing the whole camp to life with cheers that echoed down the mountain.

Mike took off running into John-John's side of the tent, dumping out all the goodies on the ground for destroying. Obadi came close behind kicking some pill bottles down the mountain. He then took John-John's hunting knife and stuck the new blade into the old canvas tent top, ripping a noticeable gash from end to end on John-John's side of the tent. The morning dew would have free access to this side of the tent, and did, for the remainder of the camp. Everyone then joined in throwing mud balls at John-John's tent, yelling savage insults as if it had been the one in the wrong. The attack didn't last long and finally fizzled. Everyone just faded back into his own individual tent, laughing foolishly and eating all the goodies the Spirits must have meant as spoils of war. Things had certainly gotten out of hand.

When John-John and Mr. Riggs arrived back at camp

later, they found the camp disturbances and saw debris laying all around one side of John-John's tent.

Everyone was sticking to the same story, saying another troop came in on a rampage. Each man was for himself. Paul said he did the best he could but just couldn't fight off everyone from all sides of the tent. John-John would have to take some losses. Everyone vowed to retaliate on another day. You could tell he was a bit hurt but accepted the story just as well, enough to get accepted into the tribe.

This camp was full of intertwining trails running all through the mountainside in and out of each campsite. They were worn in from camps past, a perfect place to set up an ambush site for newly arriving troops. Playing war games with each other was exciting only for so long. As the boy's grew tired of the game, each came to an extended resting break by the creek. Laying back under the shade, taking in the serenity, listening to the surrounding sounds of nature, the water rushing by, no one was saying a word. All of a sudden, Obadi pops up and offers his grand scheme for a great ambush.

It was almost time for supper and the plan was laid out to take place in two phases. Part one would commence when everyone was returning from their first meal. The element of surprise was the key. Obadi's gang would hurry and finish eating before the rest and rush back up the trail leading back to their camp. At a predetermined spot along the trail, they would veer off toward the uphill side of the trail.

There, they had stockpiled an arsenal of pinecones to throw down on those who passed by, their victims! Phase two would come later in the night to cover up any suspicion.

By now it was time to go down to the dining hall for dinner. A bell rang from the cafeteria signifying suppertime. Each Scout troop had to gather at their designated camp and march down to stand in line at the cafeteria. Mr. Riggs, the principal, blew a whistle to muster everyone up for the single file march down the gravel road. Obadi and the gang started a quick lookout for a prospective upcoming retaliation victim. This was not hard to find seeing how all the individual troops claimed a unique posture of who was better. Seeing the major diversity in Obadi's troop carried a great prestige. Naturally this gave something for others to shoot for, to be like those damn Indians. There must have been well over one hundred Boy Scouts from all over the country. As everyone piled in to eat and get to know each other, one of the first questions always seem to be centered around where one was from. The more Obadi listened he couldn't help but feel a little guilty. As he looked around at the other boys, from time to time he would catch a look. They too, seemed to be wondering what might transpire, so much so, that he finally had to cut one conversation short rushing up the rest of the gang to finish eating.

Scout Camp was set up like an army camp. The dishwashing station consisted of long tin washbasins lining the walls and spread down the middle. There were older boys standing on benches, shouting orders out directing how to do a good washing, rinsing, and putting trays and silverware in all the right places. It was a relief to get out of that place. Everyone shot out the screen door, screaming and running half way across the field before realizing any sense of relief and stopped to wait for the rest of the gang. Once they were all regrouped, Obadi led the way back on to the trail toward their camp. All were talking to each other about the food, which would have been pretty good if it wasn't for those older boys bossing everyone around.

At the ambush site, conversation stopped. Everyone stood still, looking around to make sure the trail was clear. All was quiet except for the noise coming from the cafeteria. At that point, the gang rushed into the hiding place and waited, and waited, and waited. Finally, someone let out a loud fart. Everyone busted up giggling till Obadi hit Mike who was the closest to him. Mike, in turn, hit Vincent who started a laughing chain reaction until voices could be heard coming up the trail. Everyone froze and listened. The voices got closer. Obadi leaned over and whispered into Mike's ear. "Pass it on to wait until I signal." Night was falling, making the trail hard to see. But, the voices kept getting louder and louder, until figures could be seen rushing by on the road, underneath Obadi's hideout. He waited just long enough for the first figure to get past him before he slowly got to his knees and yelled out a loud Cherokee war cry sending a shower of pine cones down onto the victims. The panic and chaos on the trail could be heard all the way down to the cafeteria. Once all the ammunition was spent, no one had to plan the next move. All the boys turned and raced all the way back to their camp. They were all laughing hysterically, while holding onto their stomachs. They all fell onto the ground almost in tears, crying with laughter. The scoutmaster came out of his tent asking where everyone had been. Of course the answer was obvious, "just playing!"

On the way back after dinner that night, Obadi had spotted the perfect scapegoat for phase two of the ambush. Another boy-scout troop whose campsite was sitting three sites down the road from theirs; close enough to find in the dark but far enough away for Obadi and the gang not to be blamed. That troop had a bunch of city boys like John-John. It would be like a dog killing a flock of chickens in a chicken coup.

That night after taps was sounded and all the other troops started snuggling in bed, Obadi and the gang met in one tent to plan the attack of phase two of the ambush, under two sleeping bags zipped together and using the red lens on the boy-scout issued flash lights. It was quite late in the night when they finally took off in the direction of the camp three sites down the road. Obadi would lead since his grandpa McGillis was a "Army Dawg" in the "Big War" and had instilled some of the warfare tactics that fascinated everyone. Obadi had learned things like this on many deer hunting trips he and his dad went on as well.

They walked staggered about three meters apart. Absolutely no talking would be tolerated. It would be one step at a time as they followed the streambed all the way down to just above the target camp. Easily identified by the many burning fires in each camp, you could see figures standing around some of the fires talking loudly. Once there, everyone would belly crawl up as close as possible and at a signal, all would start throwing whatever they could grab at the tents of sleeping city boys. This is how it must have felt back in the "olden days", Obadi thought.

All went as planned and the city boys didn't even realize what had hit them. They even cried out for mercy, sending Obadi's troop racing back up the mountain. John-John was left wheezing and gasping for air, somewhere near the creek. Obadi and the gang just laughed and ran on not knowing until later that night. That's when John-John finally got to camp and jumped into his nice cozy sleeping bag. He found something crawling up his leg and had a serious asthma attack. The next day Obadi and the rest of the gang spent their free time searching for and recovering John-Johns inhaler. No one bothered him after that.

Needless to say, since no one could point out the perpetrators, this one incident started a nightly occurrence spreading throughout the rest of the camps that would last the remainder of the stay. On one night towards the end of camp, Obadi's gang got caught in an ambush but fled unscathed. Yes, it was a time of innocence and exploring Mother Earth, the world around us. We were true friends for life; ready and willing to conquer the world. We were indispensable.

Canoeing

The next morning was the first day of class. No one in Obadi's troop wanted to miss it, the canoeing merit badge class. Merit badges were round, embroidered patches that were earned. They were sewn onto a sash, which was worn across the chest showing rank all the way up to Eagle Scout. You earned these by completing a number of tasks associated with a particular skill.

When everyone arrived at the lake that morning, the mist and dew were still rolling off the lake like steam created when water is splashed atop a hot pot-bellied wood stove.

The first order of business was to make sure all class members knew how to swim. A test was scheduled for 9 a.m. As anyone who has grown up in the mountains of North Carolina knows, the water is going to be ice cold.

The task was to jump in, wait for a designated whistle to be blown, swim about 25 meters out to a platform and back, and then tread water for two minutes. Easy enough, right? Well only Obadi and Mike completed the test enabling them to take the canoeing class. It seemed simple as you jumped in, but the water truly was like ice water. Everyone just wished the instructor would hurry up and blow his whistle. As you swam toward the platform, the water changed from cold to colder, then back to cold. The distance itself took your breath away. The cold, cold water took the rest. The fish hitting your feet gave at least Obadi the push needed to make it back in record time. Once back, Obadi didn't even wait, or have to be told he made it. He jumped out racing to grab a towel.

He didn't know at that time that he would be back in that dark, cold, miserable water again in about an hour for the canoeing course. They had all figured it would be an easy course. How hard could canoeing be for an "Injun"?

The first hour or so was spent sitting on cold bleachers, listening to several instructors go over proper canoeing techniques. Obadi and Mike lost interest; both started messing around tying other scouts' shoelaces together. At one point, they both caught sight of two ground squirrels playing around not too far from the class instruction. No one else seemed to pay any attention to the small animals flopping around as if showing-off. Those old Indian stories must be true. Obadi and Mike both busted up laughing, scaring the ground squirrels up a tree and drawing the attention of the whole class. At that point, the instructors got the hint and quickly wrapped up the instructional part of the class by saying, "Alright, are we ready to try this? Let's choose partners and grab a life vest, one paddle each and stand by a canoe."

As everyone started racing toward the canoes, Obadi and Mike couldn't help but trip up some of the other boys, catching the boys by surprise causing them to throw their paddles into the air, tripping, falling and piling on top of each other. If the instructor had been paying more attention, these boys would have surely been banned from the rest of the course. But they were too busy putting in their own canoe. By the time they heard the ruckus and turned around to see what was up, everyone was already laid out on the ground. Some even slid into the edge of the lake.

In the canoes, the instructor started showing individuals how to do different strokes. Again Obadi and Mike showed the mastery of their innate abilities. The instructor had to keep yelling for the boys not to stray too far out and stay with the group. I guess everyone couldn't wait for the instructor to finish. Everyone wanted to venture out on their-own. However, one final exercise had to be completed.

The instructors rounded everyone up and started lecturing on what to do if a canoe capsized. They said the main thing is not to fight it. Once the canoe is overturned, do not panic. Come up on one side and two people can simply turn the canoe upright. It may be full of water still. But you can both get in and paddle to shore. Of course, in a river you quickly learned to stay up river of the canoe and use the ends to pick up and turn over. There will be no water in it. The instructor finished by saying, "Simple enough, any questions? Good! Now comes, your final test.

Everyone get in the water. Let's turn the canoes upside down. At our command we want to see if you all can do what we have been going over. Ready? In the water!"

Now this was not in the course description. All the scouts just looked around at each other to see who was going back in that dark, cold water. Obadi and Mike looked at each other, shrugged shoulders as if to say, oh well and flipped. Boy, the water was so cold; it took more persuading from the instructors to get the rest of the class to participate.

As Obadi and Mike worked to get the canoe turned upright, each was fighting the water to stay afloat. With a lot of yelling, punching and swearing, they were able to get into the canoe and paddle back toward shore. But, the canoe kept sinking till finally they couldn't paddle anymore. Because the thing was resting on the bottom, both swam the rest of the way to the shore. After the instructor's regained composure from laughing so hard, they paddled over to the boys yelling, "What are you doing?" The test is to get the thing to shore. So back in the water Obadi and Mike went trying to retrieve their canoe. Each took turns diving down about 5 feet to touch the canoe. There was no way that two little boys were going to move that thing. It was water logged. Finally, the instructors came to the rescue. They tied a rope around the canoe and pulled it onto shore. Needless to say this took longer than it did for everyone else, making them the last ones out of the water. The instructors started scolding the boys saying this task could possibly save their lives someday; they passed the canoe merit badge requirements.

With that came the privilege of signing a canoe out any time to venture on the lake on your own. To Obadi and Mike, this meant taking out the rest of the gang.

The last class of the day was basket weaving, a task for women as far as the Indian boys were concerned. As the non-native instructor wrapped up the day's class, the boys all raced out and ran down to the boat ramp to cram into two canoes. Let's see now. Of course there was bickering over who was going ride with whom. Little Ed got first dibbs as everyone already knew he would choose to be in the canoe with Obadi. John-John wanted to get in too but Obadi chose Vincent instead, sending John-John to Mike's canoe with Paul. While Mike and his gang fought over seating arrangement, Obadi's crew kicked off the shoreline heading out to open water. Obadi sat in the back giving commands toward the front where Vincent was working hard at paddling. Little Ed just sat in the middle taking it all in. Mike started yelling at Obadi to wait up. But Obadi was in his element and no one was going to disturb his moment.

Time seems to fly by when you are caught up in the moment. This was no exception. The dinner bell came and went as twilight started casting beautiful shadows across the lake, a moment only the privileged can truly appreciate. All the while Mike and his gang kept on shouting for Obadi's attention. It wasn't until Obadi was around the spillway at the other end of the lake that he slowed down to look around and wait for Mike. By this time, Mike and his crew had worked up a clever scheme to get back at Obadi. As they pulled up along side Obadi's canoe, a war of paddle splashing erupted. Even Little Ed got into the warfare using his hand to splash water into the faces of the attackers until their canoe drifted close enough for him to reach out and grab Mike's paddle which caused an individual tug-a-war in which Mike finally had to let go before he lost his balance and capsized his own canoe. Obadi quickly used his paddle to push off Mike's canoe, pushing it into the "No Swim" zone. This area was buoyed off in a half circle around the giant spillway. Seeing what had transpired and instead of trying to save ship, everyone in Mike's canoe jumped ship, leaving him to fend for himself without a paddle. A moment passed as he looked at Obadi, who was speechless for awhile as everyone else in Obadi's canoe yelled "Paddle!" Seeing what was happening, Obadi quickly started yelling, "Jump, Jump, Jump!" Mike jumped and swam toward Obadi's canoe. Panting hard like a dog he started swearing at Obadi. Both turned around just in time to see the canoe go over the spillway. A long silence was finally broken as everyone just started laughing uncontrollably, hanging on to Obadi's canoe. After getting everyone safely to dry ground, the gang gathered on top of the spillway to view the mangled metal at the bottom of the 30-foot drop. Obadi interrupted the recount of events by asking how Mike was going to explain this. Mike retorted back that he hadn't signed out the canoe. If anyone were going to have to explain, it would be Obadi since he had signed out the canoes. Obadi thought for a moment. He had only signed out one canoe and had thought Mike was signing out the other.

Everyone reasoned that if they stayed out long enough. Maybe the canoe people would close up and go to dinner. A plan was laid out for Paul to wander around the shoreline toward the canoe take-out and wave when it was clear to return. It worked out as planned. After a day or two, no one seemed to even miss one canoe. Toward the end of camp a rumor was heard that the scoutmasters where trying to find out if someone outside of camp was trying to sabotage camp equipment. They had found a canoe messed up at the bottom of the spillway. That was only one of many predicaments in which this bunch would find themselves.

Indian Language Class

The next class was Indian lore, what a joke. In this class the boys where supposed to learn how to be like a real Indian. As it was, this class was in for a real treat, which the instructor failed to realize.

He asked Obadi and Little Ed if they would like to teach the class some real Cherokee words. Talk about being put on the spot. It seems people don't realize that just because one has an Indian name, lives on the reservation, and has a government Indian card doesn't mean you know how to speak or live Indian. Even though Obadi and his family lived on the reservation, they knew few words in Cherokee. The Cherokee have assimilated into the mainstream American culture so much it is shameful how much real Indianism has been lost. A lot of people still think if there are any real Native Americans, they must all still live in teepees. Of course, everyone has a great, great grandma who was a Cherokee princess right? Being Cherokee was none of this, but the rest of the class didn't know that. Obadi was determined not to let anyone put him on the spot.

He leaned over to Little Ed saying, "Just follow me," as the whole class watched. Obadi looked around the room and slowly began to blurt out some gibberish. Then, with a puzzled look on his face, Little Ed did the same.

The instructor was all impressed and asked, "So tell us what you said"?

Little Ed was in awe looking at Obadi with a smile. Waiting for any kind of helpful answer, Obadi spoke up fast and without much thought said, "Well.... I ah, I said Hello to Little Ed and ah.... How are you doing?" Little Ed answered confidently, "Yeah, I said, fine, how are you?" Everyone applauded agreeably and that was supposed to have been that. As luck would have it, the instructor turned to the class asking, "How many would like to learn more authentic Cherokee Indian words to take home?" Of course, they all agreed.

The instructor turned to Obadi and Little Ed and asked, "Would you oblige teaching this class a few Cherokee Indian words?"

What could they say but, "Ah, all right I guess a few words would be all right." Now the problem was remembering exactly what they had just said. This was handled ingeniously by just teaching something totally different. And they got away with that.

It sure would be funny to see one of those boys today somewhere and hear the gibberish that Obadi and Little Ed taught them, thinking it was authentic. And to think, they got a merit badge for it!

The rest of the gang left that class laughing and mocking the wording almost to the tee. Saying things like, "Boy that was something. How in the hell could you two come up with all that so darn fast?" Obadi just took off walking down the road mimicking the Indian in those old western movies, putting one hand in front of his mouth and the other behind his head like a peace sign. Bending over slightly he started skipping and bobbing up and down yelling, "Wooo! Wooo! Wooo! Wooo!"

Painted Rocks

The afternoons were left open for leisure time, that meant play time or exploring. One afternoon with a cloudless, beautiful, blue sky overhead, it seemed to be a perfect time to mess around the creek. This was a great past time on the "rez", damming up the mountain streams and catching crawdads. With nothing real exciting happening at this point in time, it was something harmless to do.

The boys came to a place hidden by steep sloping banks on each side, protected by the towering oak trees surrounding it. An unusually big rock stuck out in the middle of the stream. Sparkling clear water sort of eased past the rock, swirling just enough to notice the smooth bed of pebbles at the bottom, just invitingly deep enough to take off the shoes to wade in. Picking up the different shades of stones, looking at them awhile, and then tossing them to a new resting-place, someone could spend hours here.

This place was so peaceful and serene, no signs of pressuring "civilization", no hint of mankind, but most of all, no sign of authority just pure nature at its finest.

"This would be the perfect spot to leave our mark," suggested Obadi. At this, Vincent quickly added, "And I have just the thing", as he pulled out a black magic marker saying, "I knew this would come in handy."

Obadi was thinking more along the lines of building some kind of monument but now with this, they could all write their names on something. They could be remembered for generations to come, like when the first natives discovered writings left by the ancestors in caves. They all learn about them from old Cherokee A-yu-we-ni stories. It was a good idea, but on what and where?

Again it was Vincent who thought up the idea saying, "Hey, let's write our names on a rock and throw it in the bottom of the stream". Good idea, everyone gleamed. So they started taking turns putting each of their names on a human head sized rock that Mike found. Then all together, they lunged it into the water, making a big splash. That was that, it was getting time to head back to camp.

It didn't take long, maybe a couple of days before one of the camp officials found the rock. Sticking out like a sore thumb in the middle of this beautiful setting, with the names of all the culprits, it pointed the finger at only one troop. A thing like this upset quiet a few camp residences, as well it should. These boys needed to learn an important lesson that would be relevant for the whole camp, one the culprits should never forget.

As for the punishment, everyone elected to make the boys scrub the names off the rock, no matter how long it took. Absolutely no other activities could be attended until the completion of the punishment.

Sounds easy enough for the gang but little did they know that the task at hand would last hours on end and still not be totally complete. The morning flew by with no lunch and the afternoon seemed to be slipping by. Trees start casting their mid afternoon shadows making the deep forest frightening.

As the boys stopped for a break it didn't look like they had accomplished much. With no one around to supervise the progress, Obadi and the troop figured that no more harm could be done now. Why not take a little time out for an adventure?

As they searched the mountainside, not too far from the rock was a man-made fishpond. It was not too long or too wide, but looked deep with mega fish. As the boys looked in at the pool of fish swimming around they too looked content making do with the circumstance that surrounded them. The terrible thought of having to make do made Obadi sick to the stomach. Nothing he could do could change the sad world for the fish or for him or the rest of the gang with him. He took the blame.

If there was nothing he could change in this position of feeling stuck he could take it out on someone, anyone, here and now. The unfortunate victim happened to be Mike who was sitting with his back turned toward Obadi on top of the concrete wall surrounding the pond. Mike was waving his right hand in circular motions in the water watching the fish nibble at his figure tips as if wishing for food.

In a simple act Obadi yelled out "residents" and pushed Mike headfirst into the pond of hungry fish as he along with the rest of the gang, took flight back toward the rock. However, they only took a couple of steps before everyone had to stop to make sure it was true. Then everyone just busted up with laughter seeing Mike standing up in the middle of the knee high pond water soaked from head to toe. Not knowing exactly what had just transpired, he was looking a bit frightened and puzzled but trying to laugh along with the rest of the gang.

As Mike shivered on the bank drying in the sun, Obadi decided enough was enough. He sent Little Ed back to get John-John's new Boy Scout hatchet. When Little Ed arrived back a little while later, Obadi started to quickly chip the names off the rock. Each boy then took turns scrubbing it to make it look worn and tossed the rock back into the water.

The residents were satisfied and that ended a hard learned lesson to never leave your name on the evidence. Everyone vowed to re-sharpen the hatchet John-John donated to the cause, but I don't think anyone ever did.

Wilderness Survival

The most memorable event happened during the most important course in Boy Scouts, the Wilderness Survival merit badge class. Four days of classroom instructions followed by a two day, three night excursion up in the deep dark mountains. Alone and far away from camp, you have to hear it as told by the scouts who experienced this event with the natives.

As it turned out, the classroom portion was more of a bragging session of all the wrong things not to do. They went over things like how to start a fire using flint and steel, setting up a lean-to shelter and searching for native plants to eat or not eat, real basic stuff that all the reservation boys thought they already knew. Needless to say, the instructors seemed somewhat annoyed by the interactions and corrections the native students kept giving. The other scouts were just as put out with this nonsense. So halfway through the Wednesday class, the instructor wrapped it up by giving the requirements and expectations of the overnight wilderness survival test. Simple, survive two days and three nights out in the wilderness with only the clothes on your back, one hamburger patty, a knife and the standard issue Boy Scout flint and steel. To most, this was going to be a real test and challenge.

As the Instructors marched the class up the mountain past the last campsite, the scenery changed from a wonderland to a frightening, wild, overgrown jungle. The road got smaller and smaller up the mountain side until finally there was no road. Even farther, the trail turned left. The instructor kept going, totally off the trail into the woods. He went up and down over a couple of mountain ridges to the top of the tallest mountain around that area. Looking down into the valley, you could see the lake in the distance. Dog (Obadi) and his bunch thought this place was perfect. A small stream was just down slope and a tall pine tree stand was going to serve as the spot. The instructors would leave the troops but first he went over some last minute instructions then asked if anyone had any questions. Everyone just looked at each other shrugging shoulders. He said his goodbye in a sarcastic way, then turned and left as he headed back down the mountain, saying, "Hope to see you all on Saturday, ha ha ha."

After that, everyone just sat down taking in all beauty surroundings. A little breeze started blowing through the trees bringing everyone to their feet, that is, everyone except Snake (John-John) who just wanted to lie around and sleep. Slowly, everyone else started wandering around in search of material to start each individual's lean-to shelter or to find that perfect spot. Home for the next three nights, Mouse (Vince), Dog (Obadi), Bear (Little Ed) and Hawk (Mike) stood together looking around for a while longer when finally Snake shouts out from the ground, "What you think Dog?" Looking around more, Dog finally said, "Does it feel like it will rain June Bug (Paul)?" June-Bug swings down to the ground from a tree he had been climbing saying, "It sure feels like it." If so, I sure the hell wouldn't want to be in that steep side or down hill close to that creek." Hawk burst out laughing saying, "Rain has never killed any of us." Mouse pointed toward a flattened area more in the middle of the pine stand. He says "that's a good place for me" and heads off. Bear nods in agreement and follows suit. Dog studies the area a little more and walks a little farther up hill to a depression made from a fallen tree on the side of the mountain.

It was getting dark before everyone started mingling

around Dog's campsite. With Dog sitting in front chewing on a stick, everyone took up seats in a semi circle around him. Even the city boys were gathering around. Here in this survival situation there was no distinction of race, only one common goal for survival-stay alive. Its funny how everyone finds their position within a group; all the same qualities Obadi would find more interesting later in leadership roles.

As night started to fall upon the landscape everyone worked feverishly at trying to light a fire. Even the red skins seemed unable to get the hang of lighting a flame from a piece of flint and bar of steel. It looked easy in the film and textbook. Needless to say, everyone went to bed hungry and cold wishing now they had paid more attention in class.

Some time in the middle of the night a loud screech awoke everyone and Mouse raced straight toward Dog's camp. Dog didn't even bother coming out of his lean-to. Hawk flew to Dog's camp site also almost knocking down the shelter asking what the noise was. Dog yells out, "Screech owl, go back to sleep!" Bear is heard mumbling something in his sleep and Snake is seen coiling up on the ground. He was the only one who never bothered to complete his shelter and just fell asleep next to Dog's camp. Later on, Mouse comes, running back saying he keeps hearing something clawing the leaves near his camp. Dog points-out, it's probably a raccoon wanting to get at some of that candy Mouse had stashed away. Mouse asked in surprise, "How did you know?" Dog says calmly, "Shhh, I know you. You're a spoiled brat but we love you anyway. You are among family, man!" June Bug yells out, "Mouse has candy!" That brought everyone running up to Dogs' campsite again. Getting up, he tells Mouse, "You might as well share now that everyone knows. Before someone just takes it away from you." Mouse, of course, obliges and everyone sat around telling stories and sharing snickers bars the rest of the night. That is, until everyone was too tired to stay awake any longer.

The next morning Dog woke to find no one had even bothered to leave. They were all laid out right where they sat the night before. As everyone slowly began moving around, Dog went scouting around and came back with a couple of sticks. He made himself a miniature bow looking thing with shoelaces; only the lace was wrapped around another stick. Everyone gathered around to watch and laugh. One of the other boys muttered, "That isn't going to kill much of anything." Bear retorted back, "That's going to be our fire", as Dog pushed down one stick and rub back and forth working the other stick.

It took a little effort, about half an hour, to work the sticks. Finally, smoke could be seen getting everyone all excited. Each was trying to put his hand in to help blow, feeding the smoke into a flame. Eventually, a small fire erupted into a big warming fire. Everyone just stood around with their backs toward the flames warming. June-Bug mumbled to himself that, "Fire, it can kill, yet it can be a lifesaver. How ingenuous of man!"

Snake asked, "What about tonight? Who is willing to get the fire going tonight?" Mouse spoke up, "Shoot, we can't let this one burn out!" One of the other scouts answered back, "Well, who is willing to watch this all day?" Dog yelled back, "What else do we have to do?" The rest of the day was spent taking turns to go gather wood, nuts, and berries. Bear came back with what the Cherokee regard as a delicacy, a wild onion plant found only in certain places in the mountains, called a "ramp." The whole troop yelled in delight. June-Bug took his hamburger out and tossed it down the hill yelling, "Who needs this stuff when we have all this" waving his arms all around and encouraging the others to do the same.

Each person fixed up their own campsite for the instructors' inspection on Saturday, each individual site would be graded "pass" or "fail" for the merit badge.

Lying on the ground in mid afternoon, Dog realized this is what it must have been like before the white man came and changed society. If only he could find a way to make a living out here in the woods. That would truly make him the happiest person alive. Dog, Snake, and Bear lounged around at Dog's campsite. Just then, another great idea popped into Dog's wondering mind. Sitting up, Dog asked Hawk, "How long do you think it is back to the cantina?" Mouse quickly replied, "No longer than it took to get up here; maybe an hours walk, why?"

Dog answered, "Well, if we get started now we can be back before nightfall. And, who is going to know?" June-Bug suddenly sat up saying, "Let's get going!" Several other scouts decided to go along as well. Snake, June-Bug and Bear decided to stay back, not wanting to slow the rest down.

The walk took less time to get back down the mountain than it took walking in. Just in time to see the cantina open. For certain to deliver all the pleasures one could afford. Loaded down full of candy and pop, the journey back took longer. By the time they reached the campsites, everyone wished they could turn around and head back down to restock.

That night was much like the one before, except there was a big, warm fire. Stories were shared but the main story every scout wants to know. Is how do Indians get their names? Obadi started to get mad but simply stated how every name has a character; not something just given but something earned.

Again, everyone slept rowed up around the fire. But this night, it started to rain. When Dog finally woke up the next morning. He found everyone in his lean-to. He jumped up mumbling "what the?" With the rain still drizzling down, no one even bothered to move a muscle except to fill the empty space and keep on sleeping. Everyone put aside their differences and shared a moment of peace. Isn't this how it was meant to be?

Considering it was the last day there was not enough to satisfy the hunger in everyone's stomach. So the unspoken task for the day was to get down to the creek and find those hamburger patties now that there was a fire to cook on. It's amazing what you will do when that hunger hits you. Hamburger is good even without bread when you are that hungry.

That last night was joyful because everyone knew tomorrow they would be back to civilization and in warm sleeping bags. A step up at any rate and another valuable lesson learned; when you think you have it bad, it can get worse.

The instructors arrived around mid morning and judged each site with funny looks on their faces. However, no word was said. Each individual campsite looked clean and perfect with a fire pit in front of each campsite. Pretty impressive, only those experiencing those moments can truly say what went on up there. It was Merit badges for all.

However this is a different story of what one urban kid told his parents about the wilderness adventure when he got home;

"Mom, there were these Indians with names like: Bear, Snake, Hawk, Mouse, June-Bug and Dog. All best of friends! Dog was like the ring leader and Hawk helped him keep order. Snake kept missing around with Mouse and June-Bug which was funny to watch. Bear was neutral; he just kind of tagged along with all the others.

Until this one day Snake tore down Mouse's shelter and ate all his food. June-Bug tried to help Mouse fight Snake off but Snake was too big. So Hawk jump on Snake from behind as they rolled around they were knocking down everyone else's shelter except Dogs. Now Bear was Snakes best friend so Bear took after Hawk but Hawk was too fast for Bear. Dog which everyone knew was Bears half brother jumps Hawk as he is flying by Dogs shelter to get away from the mess he got himself into trying to help out Mouse and June-Bug who are just standing around watching with the rest of us. When all of a sudden a noise is heard in the distance and thinking it to be the scout master, they all stopped and stood up, then just end up rolling around on the ground laughing to death."

Finally a grand mother walks in yelling out to her grandson to quit making up tales and go to bed. Looking at the awe struck parents saying "my goodness, I thought you all sent him to boy-scout camp not the zoo."

Back to school

As the short humid summer fun ends, winds of change bring in fall colors and school. This was one of many precious times for Obadi, marking a beginning of new ideas and relationships; wonderment of what the future might hold. School time was a sad moment because this meant having to leave the security of family.

Living on the "Rez" entitles you to attend the BIA school in the middle of the town. But Obadi's parents, Big Mac and Elizabeth, having met in a BIA boarding school decided, as most Indian families during that period did, insisted that in order to get their children a quality education they should send them off the reservation. Instead of dwelling on the true horror stories of the past boarding school days. They would send them to one of the local public schools. Several bordered the reservation and all invited the talent the Indian students brought to the sports programs. The student body with its stereo typical images appreciated the presence the "Noble Savage" Indian brought with them. This seemed to always make the Indian students act the part. They are always walking around stiff with pride, looking tough, wild and quiet but willing to accept any and all challengers, distant and always a bit detached.

The school Obadi's family attended was a 1 hour drive each way. A school bus was furnished for the hour-long commute. One drawback to this was it meant these students had to get up two hours earlier and got home two to three hours later then most regular students. If you played sports for that school, that meant getting home some nights around seven or eight o'clock.

Obadi was too young to be thinking about that at this period in life. So, instead he occupied his riding time looking out the bus window daydreaming of the future or mischief.

One morning the bus was late picking up the students. As the morning fog rolled out over the mountaintops fading into the Carolina blue skies, the sun had just started casting shadows on the green landscape making perfect camouflage for a fight; a spit wad fight.

Everyone became fair game, no rules. Some preferred straws or ink pen tubes as straws to propel a more accurate shot. The method Obadi fancied was the bulky mouth full of all the paper you could possibly stuff in your morning breath, smelly mouth kind of style. It took longer to gob up the ammo but in Obadi's words it was "more satisfying". This meant being clever, confident and bold enough to outwit everyone else long enough to make a load.

As the game raged on, no one had seen Obadi yet and the bus was coming. Everyone filed onto the bus slowly ending the game, until the last person who was of course, Obadi. He came running out of his secured hiding place, jumped all but the last step and did a half turn stumble right into the bus driver who happened to be one of the earlier high school graduates. That made the students wonder why it was important to finish school rather than to have fun.

The bus driver pried Obadi off and sent him with a slight push toward the back of the bus yelling to everyone else, "Shut up and take your seats!" Even that couldn't stop the laughter erupting on the bus that morning.

Finally the bus quieted down enough so the bus driver, who acted like her day was already off to a bad start, could slowly move the bus. The bus sounded like it was on its last leg, straining to maintain speed. You got used to it; to the sound of gears grinding and the swearing of the bus driver.

Obadi still had all his ammo gushing in his mouth all that time. People started to ask him where had he been hiding. He had no distinctive target he wanted to hit bad enough until the bus driver's attitude got to Obadi. It reminded him of the verbal abuse his mother lashed out at him. All Obadi could do was just point at his mouth, then to the front at the bus driver. She was a big girl with black curly hair hanging down just over her shoulders. Large black framed thick glasses slid half way down her nose every time she looked up into the big interior mirror as if to hawk out her prey; the students.

The guys who had just witnessed this shook their heads and said, "Ooooohh. ssssShoot..."

Obadi had to act quickly or risk getting caught for sure. He spit the wad out into his right hand and rolled it around a couple of times. He ran the thought over in his mind then quickly stood up, which sent everyone else into a loud scream thinking they would get hit. He took aim and quickly whirled the spit wad at the back of the bus driver's head.

Fate stepped in as fate goes, the screams startled even those not informed on what was going on. This big, ugly Indian girl, named Possum stood up and turned around as if she owned the bus. For that instant, she did at least rule this bus. As she stood to see what was going on in the back, with her own government issued glasses, the spit wad smacked her loud and hard right between the eyes sending debris all over everyone and everything, like a spray; a shotgun blast.

It's funny how the screaming turned from an alerting sound to one more like a frightening tone. Everyone knew someone was surely going to die now. Poor ol' Obadi knew no one was going to stand up to Possum. He was in this by himself; nowhere to run, and God forbid if you hit a girl!

Possum took her left hand and with her pinky finger, slowly wiped off enough to see. Then she slowly walked down the aisle toward no one in particular. She didn't even have to say a word. Obadi, along with everyone around him, started to scream, "OooooOh...ssssssShoot'.....covering up for the storm of punishment. Do you want to know how it feels to be beaten up by a big, ugly, girl? A mean girl! Just ask Obadi.

Fall Burning

As the summer season ends, fall season begins. Leaves start changing colors and dropping to the ground. The bugs start to disappear and snakes hide away. Lightning bugs, also called fire-flies, come out to illuminate the dark mountainous landscape like twinkling stars. In the mountains of North Carolina, this is also the time to burn off the cornfields in preparation for next year's crop. For us kids, this was the perfect time to make forts and hiding places within the dead brown corn stalks and leaves. However, for Grandpa McGillis this was work time. If you wanted the field plowed before the first snow, you had to get rid of the dead material on top. He would always say fire did something good for the soil.

The usual routine for Obadi after jumping off the school bus was to greet his faithful-waiting dog. Then walk two miles up a dirt road to Grandma and Grandpa McGillis' house for some milk and cookies. Now that Grandma McGillis had died he still made the trip just to check on grumpy old Grandpa McGillis. Once in a while, Grandpa McGillis would be sitting at the kitchen table drinking coffee when Obadi would come whistling up the steps. Those times would be great as Obadi would pull up a chair and help himself to a Fig Newton that Grandpa McGillis wasn't dipping into his own coffee. The two would sit in silence except for Obadi saying "Mmmm" with each taste of cookie. But, those tasty moments were few and far between. Still, it was well worth the trek up the road, listening to the birds and squirrels call after him; throwing a stick for his dog to fetch. Skipping rocks off the surface of the river and seeing how many skips one could get with one throw.

Flat, round rocks work the best then it was all in technique.

After the snack, Grandpa McGillis would return to his work-shed to piddle with some new device he worked up. Obadi would wander back down to the house to round up the neighborhood boys (all relatives) for a game of tackle football. He usually got enough for a three-on-three game. However, on this day, Grandpa would meet the bus at the bus stop on Trigger, our old horse. This meant work. Grandpa and Trigger would knock down the stalks by pulling a short log through the field. We (kids) would start raking and piling up the corn stalks into huge mountainous piles. As kids, we would always make a game out of any thing to pass time or make the best of the situation. Here, we pretended these were settlements and we were wild Indians plundering and pillaging the place. The girls would choose some of the piles to stand behind and throw mud balls at us as we came running by with firing torches. They would actually try to hit us so we had to be lightning quick. Of course, there were always those darn dogs tripping you up. When finished, we would set the rest of the piles on fire and sit back and watch the blaze fade into the late hours of night. Grandpa would use this time to tell old Indian stories and how they use to set the whole region ablaze. He said it would help keep the forest open for better hunting and keep the snakes away. The animals liked it also so they didn't have to search so hard to fine food. Nowadays we can't do that. The forest is getting too thick to walk through, making us go longer distances to find a good hunting spot. However, nature and fire go hand in hand. The white man doesn't know that yet. I will have to tell you how fire was first given to our people someday.

The great thunder beings sent it to us. Grandpa went on to say Mother-earth is like an old woman. We have to continually groom her, show appreciation, and take and nurture what is offered or she will fade away. That could be said with any relationship as Obadi would find out later in life but that's another story. Obadi would remember bits and pieces of stories because it was hard to decipher Indian language into English understanding. Most of the time grandpa would start by saying something important in English next in Cherokee then he would tell us the meaning. Take the seasons for example I remember he would say the changing of seasons were important to remember:

This is how it was told to me a long time ago.

Winter *(go-la)* *Winter belongs to the North. The color for North is Blue which represents sadness, defeat. It is a season of survival and waiting. The Cherokee word for North means "cold" (u-yv-tlv).*

Spring *(gi-la-go-ge)* *The color for East is Red which represents victory, power. Spring is the re-awakening after a long sleep - victory over winter; the power of new life. The Cherokee word for East is (ka-lv-gv).*

Summer (*go-ga*) *The color for South is White which represents peace, happiness, serenity. Summer is a time of plenty. The Cherokee word for South means "warm"* (*u-ga-no-wa*).

Autumn (*u-la-go-hv-s-di*) *The color for West is Black which represents death. Autumn is the final harvest; the end of Life's Cycle. The Cherokee word for West is* (*wu-de-li-gv*).

Eventually Obadi would be overwhelmed by the darkness and drift off to sleep hugging his dog; listening to the crackling pops and hisses of the dying embers, watching the flicker flames dance away to the rhythm of a distance drum, in the confines of family. Dad would always have to carry him into the house to bed. Obadi reasoned, "Maybe that's why Grandpa never seemed to care much for me. I was always falling off to sleep in the middle of his stories. I wish I could tell him they still play a big part in my life, and I too will continue to pass them along to my family."

Part II
The Warrior Spirit

As John-John starts speaking at his retirement party he gets nervous and sweaty. He starts to wipe off the dampness around his collar and sees the glass of water next to the podium. Opting to take a quick drink of water he grabs the glass up and starts to tilt the glass up for the quick drink. Everyone patiently watching, John-John's glass reaches the point of his lips. A yellow-jacket bee buzzes out of the glass terrifying John-John to the point of making him drop the glass. John-John jumps back saying "Oh crap!" The whole area lights up with laughter as one of the helpers gets on stage to help John-John out. The young guy pats John-John on the back saying "That would be a hell of a way to start your retirement". Someone else in the background is heard saying "think of the poor bee. He about got eaten up". Everyone laughs more as John-John regains composure.

This reminded him of all the tricks played on him as a kid by his reservation friends which brought back a flash of rememberence of some correspondence letters he received from his nemesis and best friend Obadi. While Obadi was fighting in combat over seas he started focusing more on writing letters home to family and friends about questioning the meaning of life. To anyone and everyone who would oblige him with a response. These letters in actuality ended up resembling and paralleling John John's own life struggles for not only the meaning of life but with religion verses being identified as an Native. They went something like this:

To question my existence John, one must know my spirit in this life. My life begins with memories of a seven-year-old Native American boy growing up in the heart of the Great Smoky Mountains during the latter years of the Vietnam War. In our minds, my relatives and I would transform the dense, wooded mountains of western North Carolina into a humid jungle in which to conduct our warfare games. The surroundings seemed more than sufficient to re-enact what we saw on the evening news. Our make-believe tactical maneuvers would often last well into the night. The real war always seemed so distant and surreal. Remember the Boy Scouts?

The distance decreased immensely and reality hit home when one of our own became a casualty, another statistic on the news. We truly felt the effects of our country's involvement in war when my cousin was killed shortly before his tour would have ended in Vietnam. Just a few more days and he would have fulfilled his commitment to the United States Marine Corps. A war that had seemed so distant and surreal had now invaded our town, our home, my family. My cousin's death had a profound impact on my young mind at that time and would affect my life for years to come.

I will always remember every detail of his burial. It was during the winter, cold and dreary. A feeling of quiet sadness had consumed all my relatives. Most of all, I remember the Marine Corp Guards standing straight as an arrow, big and proud. They showed not even the slightest hint of emotion. They just stared ahead to an unknown distant place. It was as if each had a dark secret that no one else should dare to know. That would be one of the experiences I should eventually share hopefully, later in life.

Death is considered a bad thing in western Christianity. I learned that at an early age as my parents dragged my siblings and I along to numerous wakes held in our tiny mountain town. I am sure you have experienced this yourself. To understand death the Indian way is something else. It's more like a rite of passage, likened to another season. Death is something the elderly yearn for. The fierce warrior tribe, the Sioux, sum it up best saying "Honka Hey" meaning it's a good day to die. I know this now.

Looking back, everything seemed so innocent and far away. Nothing was bad for a kid. We were invincible and nothing could hurt us. Nightmares would even vanish and go away with a swipe of cold water. A bad dream could be forced to end the way we wanted it to. It wasn't like real life. Life is precious in the here and now. One wrong choice and like the snap of a finger, your life is changed forever. But life is viewed differently by those who have faced death in one way or another. Those are the hard lessons in life. You discover the older you get, the more hurt you have to endure. The more hurt you endure and hold inside, the colder your heart will become. I think Shakespeare said something like "to find a release from that hurt is to find love." My wise old grandma told me a long time ago the secret of surviving hurt is to find something to love. Grandma would say, "Love will cure all hate." Ah, but then I learned love can also cause much hurt.

First Love

My first love was an old black dog-named Yo-na, a Cherokee word meaning, "Bear." Why Bear? Because Obadi remembered Grandpa always reciting the Legend of why the Cherokee called the bear their brother he would always start telling something like this: *This is how it was told to me, along time ago, there was a boy who used to leave home and be gone all day in the mountains. After a while he went more often and stayed longer, until at last he would not eat in the house at all. He would start off at daybreak and did not come back until night. His parents scolded him, but that did no good, and the boy still went every day until they noticed long brown hair was beginning to grow out all over his body. Then they asked him why it was that he wanted to be so much in the woods that he would not even eat at home. The boy would reply, "I find plenty to eat out there, and it is better than the corn and beans we have in the village, and pretty soon I am going into the woods to stay all the time." His parents were worried and begged him not to leave them, but he said, "It is better there than here, and besides I am beginning to change already, so that I can not live here any longer. If you will come with me, there is plenty for all of us and you will never have to work for it; but if you want to come, you must first fast seven days and pray."*

The father and mother talked it over and then told the elders of the clan. They held a council about the matter and after everything had been said they

70

decided: "Here we must work hard and have not always enough. There he says is always plenty without work. We will go with him." So they fasted and prayed for seven days, and on the seventh morning all the clan left the settlement and started for the mountains as the boy led the way.

When the people of the other towns heard of it they were very sorry and sent their headmen to persuade the clan to stay and not go into the woods to live. The messengers found them already on the way, and were surprised to notice that their bodies were beginning to be covered with hair like that of animals, because for seven days they had not taken human food and their nature was changing. The clan would not come back, but said, "We are going where there is always plenty to eat. Hereafter we shall be called Yo-na (bears), and when you yourselves are hungry come into the woods and call us and we shall come to give you our own flesh. You need not be afraid to kill us, for we shall live always." Then they taught the messengers the songs with which to call them and bear hunters have these songs still. When they had finished the songs, the clan started on again and the messengers turned back to the settlements, but after going a little way the messengers looked back and saw a drove of bears going into the woods.
Yo-na! My Brothers!

I couldn't tell you how the dog came to the family. We had him for as long as I can remember. Yo-na was the best children's pet parents could ever hope to have. He was big enough to ride, tough enough to withstand the punishment brought on by small kids and very protective. He was a guardian; always near the children barking at all strangers. And, if you said, "Sic-him" Yo-na would tear off barking up a storm and charging in the direction we pointed.

Our family grew when I was in the third grade around 1972. My parents took in some foster kids. Remember? With the addition of new kids, my parents thought it would be a good idea to have new pets. Two full-blooded white German Shephard pups seemed to fill the bill nicely. When we first laid eyes on the tiny fur balls, we all fell instantly in love with them. They would be called Chief and Lady, a brother and sister canine team that would make a good addition to our new extended family.

But, there was a catch. If we wanted Chief and Lady, we would have to get rid of the older "reservation mutts" that had accumulated around the house. Dad was fed up with coming home and seeing new mutts running around the house every few days. To him, it meant more mouths to feed. He put his foot down and said if we wanted the new pups we would have to get rid of all the other dogs, period. This went on for some time until one Saturday morning he and my mom got into a big argument. The argument was not just about dogs but also over his drinking and staying out all night. This was no unusual thing for them on a Saturday morning. Mom finally slammed the door and left for town to go grocery shopping or something. We ignored them and continued watching our favorite cartoons in the living room.

Dad was sitting at the kitchen table on this particular Saturday when a ruckus erupted in our chicken house out back. All of a sudden he got up, grabbed a shotgun, and walked out the back door. Boom! We all rushed outside to see him reloading another shot saying, "Get on out here and help. We're going to clean this mess up once and for all."

We were all yelling, "No daddy, No". He turned around and slapped me on the head and said, "It's time to grow up and be a man." He then pushed the gun into my chest and ordered me to aim at the dogs that were busy having a feeding frenzy on our hysterical chickens. They didn't know what was going on any more than we did. Something bad was transpiring that changed my life forever. Death was in the air. Boom! After the first shot, it got easier. I started going crazy shooting everything; dogs, chickens, even the chicken house. Boom! Boom! Boom! All the other kids were yelling, crying and screaming at me. Dad finally grabbed the gun away from me, slapping me up side the head again yelling "Boy, what's wrong with you? Don't you know when to stop? Don't shoot the chickens!"

We dug a deep hole at the far end of our garden near the edge of our property to bury the dogs. They wouldn't be chasing chickens any more in this world. The last one to be tossed into the mass grave happened to be my dog, Yo-na. I cried into my pillow every night for a whole week. My trustworthy parents told all the relatives and they found it good for a hearty laugh at me. I felt betrayed by my own parents. As time went on I learned to love Chief and Lady dearly but they weren't mine. They grew with the family many years and remained throughout my graduation from high school.

I learned to take out my anger in other ways, as my dear friends will attest. On that fateful day I buried Yo-na, I learned to lock up all my emotions inside. I swore to the spirits above I would not allow anyone to break my heart again.

Army life

Well buddy, after high school graduation I attended Haskell Indian Junior College in Lawrence, Kansas on a track scholarship. The small college campus was located outside city limits and was within walking distance to the main campus of the University of Kansas. The majority, if not all, of the student body was comprised of Native Americans from various reservations across the United States. Haskell College was undeniably well known for talented runners, especially the cross-country team, undefeated for four seasons and counting. That was the influential factor that cinched my enrollment at Haskell but that's another story. It was during my college stay that I actually made up my mind to join the military.

One day in mid spring, a short, stocky, white Army

Sergeant recruiter came on campus during career day. He was looking for fresh, new, young victims to induct into the good old United States Army. He gave this sales pitch about how much money one could receive (up to $20,000 for college) and get college credit while serving only two to four years in the Army National Guard. Be all you can be! And, there was a program just for college students, customized to fit our needs. We could go to basic training during the summer term and be back in time for the next semester. Then, we could serve one weekend a month for an enlistment of three to six years, with bonuses just for enlisting! Most of us would qualify to have E-3 rank for having college credit. We would even get college credit for training (one weekend drill a month and a two-week summer camp). It was money in our pockets for playing war games. We couldn't beat that. It was an offer most of my friends couldn't refuse. We were easy prey. It meant having a reliable income to party on while attending school and having more money than any one of us had our entire lives. So, of course, five of us Indian students joined up that very day. Our fate was sealed.

We left two weeks before the semester ended so all of the teachers gave us special assignments and let us take our final exams early. We left together as part of the "buddy" system. It was part of the package, something new for the Army, so we were told.

The Next stop was, Fort Benning, Georgia. That's where we would receive basic training for our mechanized infantry unit. The sergeant recruiter drove all of us in a white government van from the school campus to the Kansas City airport. During the hour-long drive he kept talking to us about all the fun we were about to have in the next couple of days. However, his sarcastic attitude made us a little nervous.

The plane ride was a regular commercial flight with meal service. For some of us, it was the first plane ride of our lives. We were all starting to get a little antsy, talking about what might be expected of us once we arrived. Also, we discussed how we really shouldn't trust that white recruiter more than any other. After all, we weren't special to him; we were just a means of meeting his quota. How right we were!

The plane landed in Charleston, South Carolina. Another sergeant met us at the terminal. In a very relaxed fashion, he directed us to find a seat on the white school bus and wait for other flights to arrive with more recruits who would fill the remainder of the hard bus seats. We began making acquaintances and whispering to each other how it didn't seem so bad. We even joked about how the recruiters made it out to be really tough.

The seats soon filled and the bus driver jumped in and took off towards Fort Jackson, the processing station. Even there, everyone appeared relaxed. We were herded around from place to place getting haircuts, uniforms issued, and sending our personal belongings home. During periods of free time, a sergeant would come in looking for people to do various details which consisted of pulling weeds, picking up cigarette butts or cutting grass; what we called, busy work. This lasted for two weeks while we were waiting for our training cycle to start.

Then came the big day! A convoy of greyhound buses pulled up in front of the barracks. Excitement grew as processing personnel rushed around trying to get us all organized into groups. It was almost noontime before we were told to get on the buses. It was two more hours before they all started moving onto the freeway. The sun was fighting to push through the partly cloudy skies but you could tell rain was on the way.

I recall sitting next to the bus window looking out daydreaming of what might lie ahead. It reminded me of school days back home in the mountains. I had to grin to myself as I recalled the spit wad incident. I felt like a fish looking out of a fish bowl; contemplating the outcome.

How bad could it be? After all, so far it all seemed a lot like summer camp. It wasn't at all like the stories you heard in high school. I was thinking, "Heck, if I knew it was going to be like this, I would have joined up a long time ago."

After three hours on the road, we turned onto the base of Fort Benning, Georgia. My first observation was the new brick barracks three stories tall with an open concrete area underneath each one, luscious green grass surrounded the entire base. A set of pull-up bars stood in front and, a wooden sign announcing the place called Harmony Church. I did not know at that time, but this would be home for the next nine weeks. I wouldn't even be seeing my buddies for a couple of days. Buddy system meant being in the same company, not necessarily in the same platoon. Each company had about a hundred and twenty soldiers subdivided into four equal platoons labeled in alphabetical order; Alpha, Bravo, Charlie and Delta Company. Because of my last name I was placed in the forth platoon of Charlie company.

The bus jerked to a halt. The doors opened and a gigantic black Drill Sergeant came rushing in. He was yelling at the top of his lungs. "Listen up, you've got ten seconds to get off this bus, grab your own duffle bag and get into formation in front of the barracks. Now, move, move, move!" It was as if all hell had broken loose. The fading light of day seemed to symbolize the passing of innocence as we scrambled off the bus. We were so intimidated and afraid of making mistakes. We were frantically searching for our personal bags amongst the disheveled heap while another drill sergeant was yelling, "What do you think, stupid? We got all day? Get it and move, you pukes!"

I see my bag. I grab it and take off after the other recruits racing recklessly around the sidewalk to the concrete area in front of the barracks. Other drill sergeants are standing there side by side in their Smokey Bear hats looking mean as hell and sharp as nails. Some drill sergeants had recruits in the front-leaning rest position doing pushups. Buses continued to pull in and park right behind the others. Guys were getting punished and yelled at big time. Those poor unfortunate souls; I remember thinking, "Boy I sure am glad I'm not in their shoes."

We were assigned spots in the formation according to last names. This would be the spot we would remain in throughout basic training. That first formation, as big as it was, would dwindle drastically by the time we lined up for the final formation on graduation day.

We were ordered to run upstairs to the third floor. Being in the third squad of Charlie Company, we ran in order so that when we reached our bunks we would be sleeping under or above the guy we stood next to in formation. This also served well for mail call and all other important informational gatherings.

We found our bunks, quickly settled in and were about to catch a breather when a black drill sergeant came barreling in sending every one of us into a panic. He yelled out, "Gather around," and began giving us our first lesson on how to make the bunks. He then bellowed, "You all have two minutes to make up your own bunk and be downstairs in formation for chow. Move!"

Our next lesson entailed proper marching etiquette. With this newfound knowledge, we took off marching to chow. The meals seemed so good, but were never enough to satisfy our appetites. We were allowed to talk during meals but everyone whispered about what could be next. The day seemed to drag on as we prayed for nightfall. At last, it was lights out and our induction was over.

Using alphabetized last names as a roster, we all got a chance to stand fire watch. This duty involved sitting in a soft office chair in front of the drill sergeant's sleeping quarters for an hour during the late sleeping hours. The worst shift was two hours before reveille just before the lights came on (wake up call). You didn't even bother getting undressed to go back to sleep. God forbid if you were ever caught sleeping in uniform.

It seemed we would no sooner lay down and shut our eyes before a white drill sergeant would come in beating on a tin trash can lid screaming "Get up! Get out of those bunks. Move. Move. Move." This would be the norm every morning throughout basic training.

Some mornings I would automatically wake up mere moments before the lights came on. Anticipating the inevitable drill sergeant and his loud outburst, I would just lay there with my eyes closed; wishing I wasn't there. I would think back to my childhood when I was in grade school; reminiscing about cold mountain mornings lying in bed waiting to hear my dad start making noise to get the wood stove started during school days. When all I would pray for was, "Oh God please let there be snow on the ground so there won't be school today." It wasn't that I really hated school. It was just more enjoyable to sleep in and spend time with my family. Clang! Bang! Back to reality, the drill sergeant's wake up call.

Many recruits find the fitness training to be one of the most difficult aspects of the Army. I was one of the exceptions. It wasn't hard for me at all. I have always excelled in physical fitness and was fortunate to be way ahead of the average person in conditioning. In running, all the other drill sergeants would stand around placing bets on us Indians to see who would win. My talents made a lot of money for my drill sergeant and in turn, earned me special privileges.

The training exercises I disliked most were the many long, hard, dusty road marches. Don't misunderstand; I really enjoy nature hikes, especially the childhood wanderings and exploration of the rugged mountains back home. But, in this Army stuff, you can't go at your own pace and rest is definitely out of the question when you feel a little tired. To make matters worse, it seems they always ensure your load is as heavy as humanly possible to carry. Meanwhile, the drill sergeants only burden themselves with a small container of water. This particular time we were going on a 21-mile speed march, which meant we had to be at a pre-determined destination by a certain time. If we failed to reach our destination by the deadline, we would miss our ride and therefore have to turn around and march all the way back. The march required full combat gear and my MOS (military occupation specialty) was 11 Charlie dealing with mortars, the 81mm in particular. I had to wear all of the combat gear plus carry my M-16 and lug part of the mortar assembly. As the assistant gunner, I had to carry the tube that weighed about 45 pounds. In addition, each team member carried two rounds of ammunition weighing in at 10 pounds each.

One gun required a three-person team to assemble and operate it. The gunner carried the 80-pound round base plate and the sighting mechanism. He would slam the base plate into the ground and run to get the sight ready.

The assistant gunner carried the 45-pound tube barrel. He came right behind the gunner and quickly placed the tube into the base plate. The assistant gunner then turns toward the ammo bearer, grabs the aiming post and runs a few meters away sticking them intermittently into the ground for the gunner to have an aiming point. He then, runs back to listen to the radio yelling out coordinates for the gunner to adjust the sights.

The ammo bearer carried the radio, ammo, the aiming stakes and the tripod for the tube to rest on. After the tube was in place, he was right on the heels of the assistant gunner. He would set the tripod in place, getting it as level as possible. This made all the difference for the speed of the gunner to get the weapon ready to fire. All bubbles had to be level.

Everyone had to work as a team in order to have the gun up and running. The drill required set-up completion in two minutes or less. We would be marching and hear the command "Fire Mission." We sprang into action. Our time was close to one-minute-ten-seconds, give or take a few seconds every time. This was the fastest in our cycle so we were placed at the front of the formation.

Every so often, we were put through the drill. The more we did it, the more efficient we became. But, as the day wore on, the march seemed endless and the southern heat and humidity started taking its toll. Fatigue set in and we were worn-out. The relentless drill sergeants pushed us to keep up the original pace. Their persistence made all of us spitting mad but we dared not show it.

When we finally stopped for lunch no one had enough energy to eat. Our legs felt like rubber. Our feet were soaked in sweat and covered with blisters. The drill sergeant paid extra attention to this and made everyone change into a fresh pair of socks. I remember tightening the straps on my rucksack earlier to keep it from bouncing around and rubbing my back raw. It had cut the circulation off from my arms while sitting there on the ground leaning against it. I wanted to be ready to move out when the order was given so I didn't remove it. I tried adjusting the strap to no avail and ended up leaving it as it was. I was mad at the whole damned world. I closed my eyes wishing I could somehow displace myself from this hell. The drill sergeants were laughing and saying things like, "Look at those soft mommas' boys; and they want to be call soldiers." At that moment I think every one of us was contemplating how we could kill those bastards.

Since murder wasn't a viable option, we did the next best thing I guess. My best friend from Haskell and I came to differences, throwing all the anger and what energy we had left into wild blows that never really hit any target. Eventually, we both realized no one was intervening to break us apart. The drill sergeants were entertained by our antics and laughed in delight. I suppose this was a sure sign they were getting to us; breaking us down. I learned a valuable lesson that day and gained a lifetime friend.

One afternoon, just before we were to go to our next class, the drill sergeants called everyone back up to the squad bays. It sounded so urgent we all ran up the three flights of stairs to see what all the commotion was. We got through the doors, pushing and shoving because no one dared to be last, and found everyone huddling around one bunk. A recruit was lying on his back in full camouflage uniform with tears streaming down his pale face. His eyes were open and tears were running down his cheeks but he could not move. One drill sergeant laughed out loud and said in a mocking tone, "See here, look real close; this is the kind of puke this generation is producing nowadays. This is you: weak, cowards! How do you expect us to train you to defend your homeland when you don't have the will to face your own personal conflicts? No one cares about you. The sooner you accept that, the sooner we can move on from here." We never saw that recruit again. Rumor had it that the Army kicked him out that very day. Rumor also had it that he had received a "Dear John" letter and took a bunch of muscle-relaxers.

I can remember the first hand-to-hand combat lessons, the obstacle courses and the rain. It must have rained all but two weeks of my basic training. That is where I learned to live with the attitude, "it just doesn't matter." It seemed that no matter how hard you tried to wish or pray this situation to go away, it got miserably worse. The courses were established and organized to test basic skills needed to face an aggressive opponent. Hand-to-hand combat taught basic judo throws and knife techniques. Bayonet training demonstrated the use of an M-16 as an extension with basically a knife attached to the end. The obstacle courses tied it all together giving a realistic training scenario adding the physical element to it.

In commercials you see soldiers running through obstacle courses fast and hard on a clear sunny day. They're usually screaming and really getting into it. Ours looked pathetic in comparison. You learn quickly that it takes many practices to get a group of people to run through obstacle courses like that. Our first time looked more like the movie "F Troup" or an Army comedy with crazy actor Bill Murray. Soldiers were confronting some of their fears here. We had guys falling off the log crossings getting badly injured. Bayonets were getting stuck in the wooden dummies. People were tripping over their feet and getting cut. Guys were getting tangled up in the barbed wire. The drill sergeants were having a stressful day yelling at everyone. To top it all off there was at least a foot and half of water around every obstacle. The rain gates of heaven just opened up. That was an exhausting day for the recruits.

My fondest memories are of mail call. It was so refreshing to see all the different faces light up when they heard their names called for mail from family members back in the real world. Thanks! The few times I received mail I would skitter away to the only private corner I had, my bunk. I wanted my own space, just for a moment to soak up all the words I was reading. It never seemed enough to find out what was going on in a world that now seemed so far away. This would be a recurring feeling throughout my military career. On the flip side of this is the bad news letter or what is termed the "Dear John" letter. That's when you find out your significant other has taken up with someone else. It's like getting a knife stuck into your back. There is nothing you can do about it except harbor the dreadful feeling inside. I have seen many men change life directions after one of these letters. Experiences such as these reinforce the old saying, "sometimes no news is good news." This is especially true for a reservation boy finding out which family member got stabbed, shot, raped, beaten up or hearing about family members needing your financial help. Such was the case when I received the news about my stepbrother getting locked up for stabbing someone to death during a local fight. It was around this time when I found out that my parents were losing our family home. There was nothing I could do to help them any more than I already was which just was not enough this time, to help them out of this bind. I felt like I was losing hold of what I knew as my family. What was I going to do when I got out and where was I going to stay? So like any good soldier, I blocked up all feelings and marched on.

It was towards the end of the cycle when we had to pass our final medical exam and complete last minute paper work before graduation. As usual, it was raining. Like most days at basic training, the drill sergeants were devoted to making our lives even more miserable. They made all the recruits stand outside in the rain, at attention. One at a time, we were allowed to go in and complete our paperwork. I kept daydreaming about things back home, remembering how we would look out the window in our house and watch the spring rains come down. We would play hide-n-seek all through the house until mom or grandma would, "shhhh" us to be quiet and not make the thunder spirits mad. I recalled listening to grandpa out on the porch singing songs and the powerful refrain that would follow when the thunder spirits of the great fire God replied back at a precise time. Warm, pleasant memories of home took my mind off of the cold and misery everyone else was feeling. Not a word could be spoken. I became one with the rain, hearing soft thuds as the raindrops hit the ground around me; tuning into nature's symphony as it tinkled on the tin roof of the old army buildings and cascaded down the drainpipes; focusing on droplets landing in puddles. Causing waves to ripple outward; mesmerized by ever-changing patterns as it ran down the poncho of the soldier standing in formation in front of me. To Native Americans rain is good. It represents renewal of life. What did it mean here?

The end of basic training also marked the greatest test of our endurance, a series of long road marches. One was a 15-mile speed march with our duffle bags full. It was killer on the feet and back. The weather seemed to clear up on these days becoming hot and humid. You could feel the unpadded, rough single strap cutting into the front of your shoulders. The lower part of your back would burn as the weight of the load continuously rubbed the skin raw. That's why the drill instructor ensured the straps were pulled tight before we started.

Graduation

Graduation day was one of the proudest days of my life. It's a feeling shared only with those who have been there. At that moment in time one can truly understand the meaning of freedom and appreciate our country. For nine weeks as recruits we had no freedom. For instance if you wanted to go to the potty you had to ask permission, everything else was planned out. But on this day we were being reintroduced to our rights as individuals with a new outlook on life. Most guys had family members in attendance. The bleachers on the east side of the football field were full of such proud families. We Indians didn't have any friends or family to witness our accomplishment, just each other. I can remember thinking how our grandparents must have felt being forced by the government to attend boarding schools back in the early 1900's. Only here we were looking forward to getting back to school. It meant a home for me and back among our own kind but mostly for the prospective of women there.

The ceremony was pretty neat. We marched onto the field and formed into our company formation. Helicopters flew by and cannons blasted. A real army band marched in front of us. The color guard posted the Flags. Than the commander of the base stood up to the podium and gave a long speech summarizing our training. Standing at attention, tall and proud in our class A-uniforms, all I could really think about was getting the heck out of there. I could play their mental game but I held on to my own individuality; my Indian-ness! This I understood was how we as Indian people withstood so many years of abuse from the very government we now pledge to protect. However this is our land and we as Native Americans warriors fight for or along side anyone for that just cause. For us we know our indigenous ways will not be fully understood or appreciated by most non Natives so we are taught to keep it to ourselves. We practice our prayers and medicine in secret not to offend anyone. It is what is in your heart, mind and soul that makes you what you are-Indian. Standing there among the ranks I started humming to myself the ole XIT poem (XIT was a radical American Indian Movement band popular in the 70's): ***"The Indian has been out there in the ghettoes of the reservations for a long, long time. Surviving without*** *adequate food, clothing, shelter or medicine, can name but a few. In there place we have been given poverty, disease, suicides and bureaucratic promises of a better tomorrow. May your God forgive-you. The treatment of our people has been a national tragedy and disgrace. Your America has not been the land of proclaim equality and justice for all. We must now manage our own affairs and control our own lives and through it all remain to be, true Americans..."* I remember glancing up with a big smile on my face at the partly cloudy skies and wondering if it was going to rain again.

Readjusting to civilian life

After army basic training we had a few days to go home before heading back to school. Getting back into the civilian life wasn't so easy. My parents had lost all our reservation property in a political fight and had moved on to somewhere in New Mexico. It was as if I had to endure the effects of manifest destiny all over again. As soon as I got back home to North Carolina I headed straight toward my grandma's place on my dads' side where all the family members can count on to have an open bed at any time. Also, it's a place where I could go hunting right outside her back door. There were no other houses around for miles, just wilderness and streams. I was really looking forward to spending time alone. I just wanted to commune with nature and not think of life's problems. But, all my relatives decided to gather up for a big family dinner to welcome me

90

home and my plans for peace and solitude were delayed.

As the day progressed into evening family members started on their merry way. I thought now was my chance to get away up in the mountains before it got dark. As I told grandma of my plans she quickly asked if I would mind taking one of her old dogs with me. She said it had the mange and was about to die and my other cousins didn't have the nerve to put it out of its misery. I put my head down for a moment then asked for grandpa's old M-1 rifle he had brought back from the Big War (World War II). Yes a lot of my family had military experience even as far back as the Civil War where my great grandpa fought with the Thomas Legion of the Confederate Army. Grandma went into the back room for a few moments and came out with the trophy weapon. I grabbed it firmly, admiring its beauty and the history it represented. Thinking of the number of lives taken by this weapon, I put on my new camouflage army coat and grabbed some ammo off the bookshelf where grandpa had always kept them. Grandma had graciously left everything in its place after grandpa's passing some ten years earlier.

Walking out of the house, I was instantly swamped by all of my little cousins wanting to go with me. They were unaware of my mission. They just kept begging to go with me until I couldn't say "no". Instead, I gave in saying "I don't care as long as you all can be quiet and stay out of my way." Off into the forest we headed like a duck taking her tiny babies out for a stroll.

As we topped one of the mountains, I stopped in my tracks. Everyone behind me froze instantly. They were each peeking around the other trying to see what I was going to kill. The old dog's tail perked up and she ran ahead as if she sensed a kill also. Everything remained quiet for a moment longer until all of the sudden I started screaming out and racing toward the scared dog. At that moment it turned around to see what I was doing. Ka-boom! Boom! Boom! Boom! The poor dog didn't even know what had happened. All of the kids started screaming and raced straight towards home.

When I finally came into grandma's house, the adults were sitting around the kitchen table laughing. There wasn't sight or sound of a kid anywhere. Grandma asked, "What did you do to the kids? They are all hiding, scared to death of you saying you went crazy up in the mountains." I just grinned and said, "Oh, I just showed them a few Army tactics." Everyone burst out laughing again. It felt so good to be back among Family. I only wished my immediate family was here. Was I always going to be an outsider?

Going back to college was even more difficult. People seemed reluctant to try to understand what you had endured and what type of training was instilled in your brain. Sure, you see things in a different light. Everyone looks at you like you have a contagious disease or something, even your own kind of people. You find yourself slowly starting to withdraw from old friends and family. You migrate towards spending most of your free time hanging out with old military buddies. It's comforting to talk to someone who understands the situation. Prisoners of war who are released from prison must experience a similar feeling when they are set free. You know you don't want to go back where you just came from. Of course, this was right after the United States' involvement in Vietnam. The pride for the U.S. Army still wasn't felt. It was especially true for a Native American with knowledge of what history books have failed to teach about the relationship between the Army and the original inhabitants of this continent.

On the other hand, military life is everything a young Native American has been groomed for, making the mental and physical transition to military training fairly easy. It can be related to the many war games of cowboys and Indians. After growing up in the ghettos of the reservation pushed off in the desolate corners of the Americas wastelands, getting a chance to take out all aggressions through a legal and productive means is a bonus. The work hard, play hard psyche fits well with Native American thinking of enjoying everyday as if it would be your last. Remember the saying of Crazy Horse, "It's a good day to die." This can be the start of a downward spiral when mixed with the enjoyment of alcohol (firewater). Without a strong intervention of spirituality, all hope of happiness can fade like the droplets in the bottle. When you are young nothing can have more of an impact on fate, than lust. It will make you or break you in more ways than one.

College days were made for chasing girls. Not just one, but as many as you could get. Late night parties, the nightclub scene, or just hanging out down by the river with a keg of beer talking around a big bonfire; it was all in the college curriculum. Many days you could barely make it to class due to a hellacious hangover. All you could do was hang your head into your hands lying over the desk, trying not to get sick, not really caring what anyone else thought about you at that moment. This too is a downward spiral into a bottomless pit.

Being a "player" has its pitfalls too, fights over girls who don't even care about you. But if one lives by a strict code and never wavers, then very girl will follow. However, when the lies start and one lie manifests itself into another, it automatically propagates a chain reaction to oblivion. Just as my mother would always chastise me with the phase like "that world is always negatively predictable". After all, aren't these facades of dances what plagiarized the concurring of Indigenous Nations to fall to ruins in the name of God or as Westerners put it manifest destiny. This is what I learned in school. Don't get me wrong. Not only do men try to master this in corporate America; women are just as bad in individual relationships.

A Player

In the fall of 1985, one player got his hand called by another at the same game. After a late night of drinking and spending the night with a one-night stand, I walked into my apartment to find the bedroom door locked. I was sharing the apartment with my beloved room-mate/girlfriend at the time. Scared voices were conversing on the other side of the locked door. Like the tale of the big bad wolf, I screamed out, "Open the door or I'll bust it down!" only to be denied with the sound of shuffling feet on the other side. Again, I yelled out, "Open up. I know you're in there. Who's in there with you?" This time I was told to go away. Like a raging bull, I rammed into the room shoulder first, splintering through the door only to get a glimpse of my best-friend and school mate making a mad dash towards the bathroom grabbing whatever clothing he could lay his hands on. He slammed the bathroom door just as I was about to get my hands on him. My girlfriend starts screaming at me to get the hell out of there or she will call the police. I turn and push her on to the bed as I ram into the bathroom door. I busted through just in time to see the fleeing feet disappear out the bathroom window. By the time I get to the broken window and stick my head out I can see a half naked body racing down the back alley stumbling around trying to get dressed.

In dire straights, I call home only to receive the news that my parents have financial problems of their own. They have lost another home in New Mexico.

Distraught, I head straight to the bus depot and catch the next bus to Albuquerque, New Mexico where another girlfriend lives. I left everything I own back at the other apartment.

Staring out the window on that long bus ride I keep daydreaming about my days of riding the school bus back in North Carolina; wondering just how many seasons I will experience on a bus. Day turns into night and I continue my vigil, silently staring out of the bus window, dreaming of the day I can finally do whatever I want. I crave adventure! I don't want to have to depend on anyone for financial help. About the time I have myself convinced of what I want, I always recall the beatings and verbal abuse inflicted upon me by my mom. These negative thoughts wash away all my dreams of a bright future. Her one saying always rings out in my head during these times. "You play with fire, you get burned by fire!"

She also knew how it felt to have that illusion of love broken. But, she stuck it out for the kids and stayed with my dad. I had to admire her for that. Of course, that was the old traditional way of doing things. However, she couldn't help but turn that rage toward someone else. Ole Obadi just happened to be the one in the way. Could this be the problem I have staying in any relationship? Perhaps some dreams of finding that perfect love just aren't meant to be shared with anyone. For some reason this whole situation reminded me of the famous Cherokee Legend of Spear finger it goes something like this: *This is how it was told to me a long time ago. Long, long ago*

96

there dwelt in the mountains a terrible woman monster, whose food was human livers. She could take on any shape or appearance to suit her purpose, but in her right form she looked very much like an old woman. But not an ordinary woman: her whole body was covered with a skin as hard as a rock that no weapon could wound or penetrate, and on her right hand she had a long, stony forefinger of bone, like a spearhead, with which she stabbed everyone to whom she could get near enough. She would enter a house by taking the appearance of one of the family who happened to leave home for a short time, then she would wait for her chance to stab someone with her long finger and take out his liver. She could stab him without being noticed, and often the victim did not even know it himself at the time--for it left no wound and caused no pain--but went on about his own affairs, until all at once he felt weak and began to die gradually, because Spear-finger had taken his liver. When the Cherokee went out in the fall, according to their custom, to burn the leaves off from the mountains in order to get the chestnuts on the ground, they were never safe, for the old witch was always on the lookout, and as soon as she saw the smoke rise she knew there were Indians there and sneaked up to try to surprise one alone. So, as well as they could, they tried to keep together and were very cautious of allowing any stranger to approach the camp. But if one went down to the spring for a drink the group never knew, but it might be the liver eater that came back and sat with them.

At last a great council was held to devise some means to get rid of Spearfinger before she could destroy everybody. The people came from all around, and after much talk it was decided that the best way would be to trap her in a pitfall where all the warriors could attack her at once. So they dug a deep pitfall across the trail and covered it over with earth and grass as if the ground had never been disturbed. Then they kindled a large fire of brush near the trail and hid themselves in the laurels, because they knew she would come as soon as she saw the smoke. Sure enough they soon saw an old woman coming along the trail. She looked like an old woman whom they knew well in the village, and although several of the wiser men wanted to shoot at her, the other interfered, because they did not want to hurt one of their own people. The old woman came slowly along the trail, with one hand under her blanket, until she stepped upon the pitfall and tumbled through the brush top into the deep hole below. Then, at once, she showed her true nature and instead of the feeble old woman there was the terrible Spearfinger with her stony skin. Her sharp finger reached out in every direction for someone to stab. The hunters rushed out from the thicket and surrounded the pit. They shot as true and as often as they could. Their arrows struck the stony skin of the witch only to be broken and fall useless at her feet, while she taunted them and tried to climb out of the pit to get at them. They kept out of her way, but were only wasting their arrows when a small bird, the titmouse, perched on a tree overhead and began to sing "un, un, un." They thought it was saying u'nahü', heart, meaning that they should aim at the heart of the stone witch. They directed their arrows where the heart should be, but the arrows only glanced off with the flint heads broken. Then they caught the titmouse and cut off its tongue, so that ever since its tongue is short and everybody knows it is a liar. When the hunters let it go it flew straight up into the sky until it was out of sight and never came back again. The titmouse that we know now is only an image of the other. They kept up the fight without result until another bird, the little chickadee, flew down from a tree and lit upon the witch's right hand. The warriors took this as a sign that they must aim there, and they were right. Her heart was on the inside of her hand, which she kept doubled into a fist, this same hand with which she had stabbed so many people. Now she was frightened in earnest, and began to rush furiously at them with her long spear finger. She jumped about in the pit to dodge the arrows, until at last a lucky arrow struck just where the hand joined her wrist and she fell down dead. Ever since the chickadee is known as a truth teller. When a man is away on a journey, if this bird comes and perches near the house and chirps its song, his friends know he will soon be home safe.

Cold Streets

It was a cold Monday afternoon in December as I wandered through the streets of downtown Albuquerque, New Mexico. The wind was bone chilling cold, blowing paper and other trash across the streets. A beer can rolled in front of me. As I was about to run across to the other side, I stopped momentarily to look down at the empty can and found relief in kicking it as far as the wind would let it fly. Running on across the street, a driver honked his horn as I jumped onto the curve. I threw up one arm and finger giving the busy man a polite wave. Aye!

I had just given up on finding a job on this day. I leaned up against the wall of one of the many tall lifeless buildings, wondering what my next move would be. I noticed the recruiting station sign just down the street from me. Kicking off the wall I thought to myself, "What the heck! It couldn't hurt to see what they have to offer".

As I entered the office I noticed that there was no one around. The place was empty. A sign on the front desk read, "Be Back in a Few." So, I took a seat and started thumbing through some Army magazines. I soon realized they never show the harsh reality and emotional pain of the experience. The more I looked at the pictures, the more negative I felt about being in this town. But something had to be done or I was destined for the streets, thinking to myself how ironic bad relationships always seemed to center around money, or lack thereof. Just as I'm leaving, I look out the window to notice a Marine recruiter walking by in his dress blue uniform.

I get up, saying out loud, "Now that is what I am

talking about." I throw the magazine back on the table and head toward the door. As I reach for the door handle, an Army recruiter opens the door just as I push by. The Army recruiter hastily states, "Hey blood, how can I help you?" I don't even bother to return a reply and rush on into the Marine office. Meanwhile, the Army recruiter is watching helplessly.

A Marine sergeant is sitting straight up at his desk as I come plowing in through the glass door. Posters line the wall and the floor is shining in the afternoon sun. The Marine sergeant quickly stands to his feet sticking out his hand for a firm handshake saying, "Come on in young man. Take a seat. Take a seat. How can we be of service to you today?" I quickly take a seat in a wooden chair and begin to talk to the Marine.

The Marine sergeant listens intently to every word before opening his mouth. The first words out of his mouth were; "Now, the Marine Corp isn't for everyone out there. We are proud of our slogan 'the few, the proud'. It's hard but when you make it you join a brotherhood." That was the selling point for me. Everything else the sergeant said was null and void. All I wanted and needed right then was to feel a sense of belonging to something in this world.

This Marine sold the organization so well that he actually had me signing papers and agreeing to an enlistment date only five days away. I was so motivated that this was all well and fine. The sooner the better!

Needless to say this ended my quest to find a job in Albuquerque this cold, lonely, winter day. It opened a new door for adventure, making me feel excited at the possibilities of finding new direction in life. I now had a purpose to continue the struggle for life and a way out of this present situation. Snow started to fall all around blanketing the landscape of New Mexico, slowing the pace of the city streets and making the mood of the situation seem a bit brighter.

Enough to want to celebrate with my kind, this led me straight to the local Indian bar located on central avenue called the Blue Spruce bar. The bar was in a rugged old building with graffiti painted on the walls and no windows making the interior very dark. There was a small dance floor at one end and two pool tables at the other with an old looking western bar in the middle.

As soon as I walked up to the counter to quench my thirst someone at the far end yells out, "Hey young blood, don't I know you? Didn't you go to school at Haskell?" That's all it took to entice a whole night of partying and taking drink shots. I partied to the point where I accidently passed out at one point only to be woken-up by the lady bartender saying, "Hey sweety, it's closing time." This snapped me back to life as I looked around and saw everyone filing out the doors. I stumbled out the back door into the dark empty parking lot. Well, empty except for this one pick-up truck doing doughnuts at the far end of the parking lot. People were hanging out of the truck cab screaming the usual "Ya-hoos!". I didn't know them nor did I want to chance a fight on a night like this. So, I stumbled on down the isolated streets. Eventually, I remember coming up to this maze intersection of railroad tracks and several streets cris-crossing each other with a set of flashing red lights. I remember thinking "now this is kind of like my life's existence. What to do?".

As I stood there contemplating when to cross, a car comes down one end of the street and pulls into the center lane as if to make a turn. The lights weren't working properly and just blinking so the normal protocol was to stop and go. But, that car just sat there still, with the music blaring. After a long pause I looked up and down the street and seeing no other cars approaching I simply walked over one set of lanes up next to the car and looked in. There sitting in the seat was a drunk lady with her man next to her both passed out cold. I knocked on the window a few times trying to wake them up to no avail. So looking up and down the streets once more and knowing how far I had to go I figured why not help them out. I opened the door and tried waking the couple up again. It was of no use. As I checked the streets I saw a police car turning onto the street at one far end several blocks away. Even though it turned the other way, I figured it was time to take some action here. So I gently push the couple over a bit and squeezed into the driver's seat putting it into drive and off we went. Did I mention I was drunk, so I didn't know where I was going, but I was sure glad for the ride.

Anyway, sometime in the early morning hours the lady woke up and started questioning me of how I got there. I simply told her the truth and low and behold she started loving up on me, feeling my leg and everything. At this point we were way outside of town, four-wheeling the many sand dunes when she noticed the gas gage. She suggested that maybe we should get some more gas. I drove the car to the nearest gas station and pulled up to a gas pump. She wanted me to pay for some gas but I had no money. This was no problem as we get out and she digs around in her old man's pockets and comes up with a few dollars. I gas up the car and she goes inside to pay. When she comes out she gets into the driver side as if she had been driving all along and starts to drive as I get into the back seat. This was fine until her old man starts to come to and seeing an Indian in the backseat of his car he starts asking her who she had picked up. They got into a big argument that led to a fight which led to us wrecking into a light pole in the middle of some street. No one was seriously injured but they kept on arguing and fighting so I simply got out and walked across the street just in time for the city police to pull up behind the wrecked car. The sun was coming up as I walked back toward the city. Yeah, I was ready to leave this place.

The Marines
Boot-camp

My thoughts changed just as the coming of seasons after jumping off that commercial plane in San

Diego, California, the home of the United States Marine Corps Recruit Training Depot. It was early January and the start of a New Year, a perfect season for change as the recruiter put it. As the plane touched down on the San Diego airport runway I just happened to be sitting next to the window and had a full view of the Marine Corps training base. Activity was bustling with formations of all kinds in plain sight. Men were exercising in bright red shorts and yellow t-shirts. Some were doing various obstacle courses, while others were in groups doing physical exercises.

A Marine sergeant dressed in his brown Marine uniform was waiting for the new recruits at the gate in the airport. Holding a clipboard, he started greeting each of us by last names and ushering everyone onto a waiting olive drab green bus. Shiny clean with the eagle, globe and anchor emblem, it gave the appearance of pride.

No one on the bus spoke a word as it slowly filled up with solemn passengers. The tension was high as everyone sat in silent anticipation. Looking out the bus windows, watching the freedom of others passing by reminded me of home, wishing I were one of them instead.

Finally, the Marine sergeant briskly climbed aboard quickly pulling the door latch and locking out the last traces of freedom, as we had known it. Leaving the airport made me feel like turning back was not an option.

The bus turned into a series of curves and slowed to a stop at a guarded gate. Two mean looking, well-groomed uniformed Military Police (MP) guards were dressed in tight brown uniforms with two red stripes on the arms, shiny black belts with a .45 caliber handgun and multicolored ribbons on their chest. One guard stepped onto the bus, took a quick head count, then reviewed the paperwork handed to him by the driver. In a monotone voice he said, "Very good!" As he turned to get back off, the other guard gave the driver a hand signal to proceed on through. That's when the real feeling of no turning back hit me.

Smoky Bear Hats

The bus pulled up in front of this monstrosity of a building complex with no windows. There were two glass doors on one side and a concrete patio in front. I noticed yellow footprints painted on the patio. The driver slowly stopped the bus, turned off the engine, exited without saying a word and disappeared into the building complex. We sat and waited. Minutes tick by and there are still no signs of movement from inside. We begin to wonder if maybe we were supposed to have followed him. Some of the guys in the back of the bus begin to whisper to each other. Several more minutes pass, then all of a sudden the two glass doors burst open. Four well-dressed Marines with smoky bear hats pulled down close to their eyes walked briskly out of the entrance, two abreast and in step, heading straight toward the bus. Reminded me of two things; one was the symbolism of the Smokey Bear hats and how as kids we would always wonder why Smokey Bear whenever he visited our school on fire prevention day, never took his hat off indoors like the way we were always being yelled at do in the south. The other thing was how these men reminded me of my cousins burial when I was a kid.

In what appeared to be a well-rehearsed move, one marine climbed onto the bus as the other three stopped in unison, pivoting and taking positions just outside the doors. Without missing a beat, the one on the bus quickly introduced himself so fast no one actually had time to comprehend his name. He continued, "Listen up! You all have two minutes to get your butts off my Marine Corp bus and on those yellow footprints on the sidewalk! Understood?" We all burst out, "Yes sir!" He quickly corrected us with a shout; "It's sir yes sir!" We sang in unison "Sir Yes Sir!" He looked at his watch, "Thirty seconds already gone, Move it!" Everyone started uncontrollably rushing past him, scrambling to get off of the bus, fumbling around like a bunch of kindergarteners. The other drill instructors started grabbing recruits, pushing them to the ground yelling and screaming into their faces, making them do push ups or jumping jacks. That's when I appreciated the seating position I had gotten. We learned from the mistakes of the first bunch and the rest of us quickly ran to the yellow footprints as instructed. We dropped our belongings at our feet and stood at attention staring straight ahead hoping not to be the one to attract attention. After a few intense moments, the same drill instructor that had yelled at us to get off the bus came to the center of the formation. The others quickly took up position in a perfect line behind him as he began to welcome us to his beloved Marine Corps Recruit Training Depot.

Darkness came, it was getting late and the marine was still speaking. I remember comparing it to my Army days thinking this can't last too much longer.

We were finally escorted into the building with more yelling and screaming. The first order of business was haircuts. A steady stream of Marine wannabes filed through the doors emerging almost immediately on the other side with shaved heads. When it was my turn, I could see why. There were eight barbers competing as if they were in a sheep shearing marathon. The first pass of the hair trimmer was always right down the middle of your head. A couple more around the sides to finish it up, a slap on the back and you were peeled. If you tried to get a quick look in the mirror the drill instructor would snap at you to get a move on. Assembled back in formation you noticed that the guy in front of you didn't look at all like he did on the bus. Everyone's battle wounds were clearly visible. Some heads were comical with all of their marks and scars.

Next, we were herded into another area of the same building to do paperwork and on to another room to turn in our personal belongings to be mailed back home. We proceeded to get physicals, clothing, boots and any other items of necessity. The routine continued throughout the night with the drill instructor barking orders non-stop.

When we finally emerged through the front glass doors, it was morning. The Southern California sun was just starting to cast bright radiant beams over the yellow and brown landscape the buildings made. The clear blue sky showed promise of a good day. For what, I would have no idea. One thing was certain. I had survived the first onslaught of pain and ridicule. This was not like the Army at all.

Standing in formation on the painted yellow footprints, we were now beginning to look like a combat unit. We were still a long way from being called a Marine but the transformation was definitely emerging. We were not allowed to tuck the bottoms of our new camouflage pants into our stiff new boots. We had to keep our sleeves rolled down and the collars buttoned up around our necks. Our new caps bore no resemblance to the traditional pressed out Marine field cap. In fact you wouldn't even dare be caught out on the street looking the way we did. The drill instructor, we found out the hard way, did not like to be addressed as a drill sergeant like in the Army. We were there to learn how to be a big, bad, rough, and tough, green, fighting machine; a U.S. Marine. It was evident nothing was going to be given to us unless we earned it through blood, sweat, and tears. Even our dress wouldn't be completed until we earned the look.

With that said we got our first lesson in commands; to come to attention, turn and march as a group. As the drill instructor yelled out, "Listen up! Ah-tent-chon! Right! Face! For-ward! March! Left! Right! Left! When I say left your left foot strikes the deck!" Just the command in his voice made us proud to be among them, the initial brotherhood.

Breakfast was, eat and run. The entire company of 120 recruits was in and out of the chow hall in ten minutes. After receiving our food we had two minutes to eat and leave. A drill instructor actually timed us and watched to see if anyone dared to talk. Of course, there was always someone messing up. This would become the routine throughout boot camp, a habit many take with them the rest of their life.

Time passed fast from that point because our whole existence was preplanned. We had a hidden agenda covering every waking moment from the time we stepped off of the bus until graduation from boot camp.

Pride was the primary focus in every aspect of being a Marine; be it in physical fitness, appearance, knowledge, history, standards, what have you. Everything had to be perfect.

Our barracks were three-story block fortresses with windows spanning the entire building. Located through the double metal doors in the middle of this building was a large open space that served as our classroom for many sessions. The hard surfaced floors were waxed and buffed to an impeccable shine that would reflect the florescent lighting making it sparkle underneath the rows of perfectly lined bunk beds. Wooden, boxes (foot lockers) rested at each end keeping all our personal gear secured. This area was referred to as the "squad bay". The drill instructor had an enclosed office space up front. He had a perfectly made bed in one corner and a desk in front of a window facing the interior bunks. The window blinds were closed. The bathrooms were situated at the back corner next to the drill instructors office and the classroom area.

In front of the barracks was a road that enclosed the infamous parade grounds where the majority of our boot camp training took place. Marching was a big deal. Later on, I realized it taught us important lessons in discipline, group cohesion, command and control.

Every day was difficult both mentally and physically. Each moment was a matter of survival of the fittest. Unlike the Army experience I had previously, around here there was absolutely no laughing and grinning unless you could find some reprieve in someone else's misfortune of misery. Native Americans have always been good at finding something hilarious as a way of coping with all the misfortune of reservation life or being in a bad situation. The use of our sense of humor helps keep the mundane tolerable and less stressful. Everyone here was hard core and dead serious. So the saying "It Just Doesn't matter!" fitted well in this situation.

There was one incident that my boot camp buddies always seemed to bring up. Every Marine has one ridiculous funny thing that sticks out from all the torture we endured. There's always one person that all of the drill instructors love to mess with. I would later see the importance of this tactic as the war philosopher Sun-Tzu states, "putting dissention among the troops can build group cohesion."

Tex

In our platoon there was a guy from Texas named Porter. We nicknamed him "Tex." He was a big good ole boy/cowboy, as friendly and good-natured as any. There wasn't a lick of bad in this kid. Tex was tough as nails, just not too bright.

One day we were marching around many endless hours on the parade deck constantly going over the manual of arms and movements getting ready for our final parade inspection. Old Tex could not get down the difference between his right and left. As the drill instructor sang out the command of, "column right," Tex would turn left, running into the oncoming people trying to make the right turn. His confusion would trigger a fury of screams from other drill instructors just waiting for these kinds of mistakes. They would stop the procession and send us back to the starting point to begin over again and again throughout the day. The next time we started, the drill instructor would yell out, column left!" There goes Tex turning right and the accordion procession of recruits piles up once again. About this time the drill instructors would pull Tex out of the formation and drag him over to the "sand pit" cursing. This is where his punishment would take place which was an exercise called the bend and thrust. He would always come back sweaty and rejoin us having to play catch up on any new instructions we had received. The drill instructors would order us to get Tex up to speed.

One morning the drill instructors yelled out for everyone to "fall out on the road for chow." We started the usual shuffle out the door with all of us racing not to be the last ones. Everyone dreaded to hear the one word command "SSStop!" The last ones that didn't make it to their designated spot would have to freeze where they were with the whole platoon resonating in unison "Freeze, private, freeze!" The next command for those that did not make it to the formation would always be in a slow calm matter, "Just get on down!" The unlucky few would have to do fifty push ups before rejoining the ranks. On this particular morning after everyone had done his punishment and was getting in line, the drill instructor was about to say "Right face!" to march us to chow. All of a sudden old Tex races out buttoning up his pants and not wearing any headgear. The drill instructor doesn't say a word for a moment. He looks down at the ground then says, "Hold up there killer! What the hell are you doing?" Tex didn't seem to know how to answer correctly so he simply snapped to attention and screamed out, "Being a lean, green, fighting Marine, Sir!" The senior drill instructor walked towards him saying, "Wrong answer!" By this time the whole platoon can't keep any composure and we fall out of line dying of laughter. The senior drill instructor became angrier yelling at the top of his lungs, "Shut up!" He got right up in face of Tex, lowered his voice and in a calm monotone voice asked, "Do you despise me?" Tex replied. "No sir! This recruit loves his drill instructors." The drill instructor quickly snapped back, "Well we hate you and everything about you. Now either you conform to our ways or I will personally kick you in the ass back to wherever you came from. You understand me, recruit?" Tex answered in an even louder voice, "Yes sir, this recruit is going to make his senior drill instructor proud!" The drill instructor turned away saying, "Just shut up and get into the pit!"

When we marched back from chow there was Tex in the sandpit digging a fighting hole with nothing but his cover (his hat). When we completed morning parade drills and lined up to go to lunch, there was Tex filling back up that hole he had been digging all day long with his cover. At lights out he finally came in looking tired but not worn-out. I started thinking that guy may not be too bright but he sure has determination. Weeks later, we found out it wasn't so much determination as it was this was all he had left in this life. Kinda like me, we all would eventually find out from each other that most Marines all had this one common trait. We were all misfits, a Marine tradition. This was my family now.

All these acts old Tex was being punished for kept the morale of the whole platoon spirited and high. We couldn't help but feel a little remorse for the guy. I did, so much to where I was compelled to write and share these funny new events in my life with several people. You may remember? On one of the Sundays when we were allowed to write home, I picked up pen and pad to jot down a few details of how Tex made us laugh. The person I chose to send this particular letter too was one of our childhood friends Vince. I was told he kept asking my mom to have me get in contact with him. In our correspondence I concluded that this Marine stuff wasn't that hard and that he should think about joining if he needed an escape. Destiny? This I would not ever forgive myself for doing.

Graduation

Sixteen long grueling weeks of hard lessons learned came to a climax on a clear bright sunny California Sunday morning. That final march around the parade deck executing all the movements we had mastered into expert precision brought a great sense of pride. Hearing those closing comments proclaiming us as "Devil Dogs" summarized our achievement. It is a name proclaimed to the Marines by the Queen of England during World War I for saving France from the German invasion. The amazing thing was how the drill instructor totally changed his demeanor after the closing ceremony, even offering to buy us all, a beer. But I was focused on getting on that noisy airplane, that we heard every night in the barracks, homeward bound. It felt good walking proudly through the massive airport crowd as everyone turned to look at us. I was now what most can only dream about, a bad ass United States Marine.

Over Seas

As luck would have it, my first duty station would be a year-long tour in Okinawa, Japan. It was a strategically placed military base on a tiny island south of mainland Japan. Home to the 3rd Fleet Service Support Group of the 3rd Marines (3rd FSSG), rumor had it that this place was a tough place to be. Being so far from the United States, rules and regulations were even more-strict here. Also, being hosted by a foreign nation, it was imperative we conduct ourselves in a respectable manner.

For the young service men and women just getting out of high school and being so far away from home this spelled disaster waiting to happen.

I will always remember the bus ride from Kadeena Air Base, the main airport we flew into, riding on a olive drag green bus through the narrow winding road of the Island to the Marine base called Camp Hanson. The first noticeable difference was how little everything was. The roads, cars, shops and even the people seemed to be on a smaller scale. A different smell permeated the air. It was continuously hazy as a result of the very high humidity. Concrete was the most prevalent construction material.

Approaching the guard gate, I noticed a machine gun positioned just to the inside right of the guard shack. A ten-foot barbed wire fence stretched around the entire perimeter as far as the eye could see. Inside were barracks, vehicles and the usual activities distinguishing it as any other military-base.

A young MP boarded the bus to check our military IDs. He continued through towards the rear insuring every ID photo matched the face of the ID holder. Without saying another word he jumped off the bus and saluted, giving us the go ahead to enter.

The bus slowly maneuvered through the outlying streets of the base towards the center. Lining the central street we saw another entire company of worn out looking Marines sitting on their field gear in rows of four. They had served their tour here and were waiting to leave for home.

As our bus pulled up behind other buses, all the waiting Marines started touting us with catcalls cheering "New-bees!" That welcome would be our ritual a year from now, when I was surprised to see someone I recognized. It was Vince. He had decided to join several months after I had written him that letter urging him to do so. He was coming and I was going back to the States. I will always remember seeing him getting off that bus as he ran up to me saying, "Hey Dawg."

Being in the fleet Marine force was tough at times. We spent a lot of time in the field. It would never fail to rain just as we headed out and would stop as we returned. True to the name, Marine training stops for nothing.

Iceman

The Japanese people didn't like us occupying their land and bringing our customs to corrupt their way of life. I could relate to them from my own Native heritage. But here and now I was a Marine wearing the Marine uniform and they treated us as such. So we did what could be expected of people that get rejected. We got drunk as skunks and tore-up things.

I met one of my best buddies as a result of this kind of behavior. His name was Iceman, a Native from Alaska. One night another neutral friend introduced us to each other at a bar full of Philippino dance girls. We both got pretty toasted, and it was into the early morning hours when this other drunken Marine came in trying to bully his way around changing the music. Since I was the regular there and Momma-San pretty much trusted me around her girls, I reached over the bar and changed the music back. As I settled back in my barstool to continue my conversation with Iceman, the newcomer slammed me in the back of the head with a beer bottle. The impact knocked me off the barstool onto the floor.

Before I could get back to my feet Iceman had leaped up doing a roundhouse kick to the drunk Marine's big, fat head knocking him out cold face down on the dirty floor. When I got up, I looked at the guy lying on the floor and did my own kick to his head to finish it up. Momma-San shooed us away through the back door just as the Japanese Police entered.

Out back we finished our beers laughing about the incident. But the laughing turned into hard core joking as he kept insisting that I got cold cocked as well. The argument was so intense that we finally squared off and brawled for about fifteen minutes until a passerby interrupted us by yelling at us "Crazy Yankee! Go home!" We stopped, shook hands, dusted ourselves and walked off hugging each other staggering toward the base. Suddenly, out came that drunk-Marine bumping into us saying, "Did you all see a bunch of guys come running this way?" In unison we both pointed down the street and said, "Yeah they went that way." The bloodied, drunken Marine took off in that direction so we went back inside to say we were sorry to the Momma-San. We became best of friends ever since that night.

The Mark

One night, while partying with Iceman toward the end of my one-year overseas tour of duty in Okinawa, we struck up a conversation about the brotherhood of the Marine Corps. We wondered if we could actually trust a white guy to protect our back in combat. That was a question we couldn't really answer. If it came down to it, we decided we really didn't want to put it to a test. One thing was for certain, we had proven our trust in each other on more then a few occasions around here. I shared how we probably wouldn't even remember each other once we got back stateside. I told him how all my Army buddies swore to stay in touch and how I hadn't heard from any of them since we went our separate ways following basic training.

To make a pact to stay in touch, we decided to tattoo ourselves the natural native way; a burn mark. We got some wire and shaped it into a "C" standing for the Corps. After heating it up red hot with a lighter, we placed it on our left forearm swearing always to stay in touch. This was the foundation of our own Native brotherhood, one that every other member in our company (Indian or White) wanted to emulate.

Chief

It rained and rained over there and if it wasn't raining it looked as if it would. When the skies were clear, it became so hot and humid that the only thing to do was to stay indoors or find some shade, wishing that it would rain again. You could count the number of clear days that year on one hand.

That is the one element that finally broke me down. It wasn't the Marine doctrine or tough persona but rather the harsh weather conditions. On one 45-day field training exercise, our company was staged up at the northern part of the island in a place called the northern training area (NTA). This is where the Marines put on the infamous Jungle Warfare Training. We had a one-day road march to get to the area and had to simulate war tactics along the way. This also meant once there, we lived in trenches and fighting holes we had dug for our defenses. I mean it was hard to dig with your hands numb to the bone and cold from every inch of your body soaked with red mud.

It was at this training area where I ran into a buddy from home. Everyone called him "Chief", he was not very tall but about as round as he was tall and looked mean as a snake. I could tell this was the kind of person the Marine Corps loved. Only this Chief wasn't too good at taking orders from any one period so he was busted down to private and was always on restriction for something or another. Boy did he love his drink. I was sure glad he knew me and liked me. I could truly count on this guy to die for me. I would have to thank him someday for setting me up with all his contacts over there. But on this day he just laughed out loud saying "It just doesn't matter! You just gotta love this shit!" But I refused; the more I tried to push this misery out of my mind the more it hurt. About all I could do was just slump down on the ground in a sitting position; legs stretch out in front of me, spread open into a V. I started slamming the muddy earth with my fist. It was Chief who came up on along and took up a sitting position like me and started doing the same thing. I couldn't help but forget my troubles and row backward laughing.

One night, as I stood guard in the rain, it just wouldn't let up. I huddled under my poncho the best I could, scanning the jungle landscape as my hole filled with rainwater. Cold, wet, and hungry I started thinking about home; questioning why I was doing this. A snake slithered across my arms just in front of my face. Thinking of home this reminded me of the Cherokee story grandpa told about the great snake called Uktena. I started reciting to myself trying to mimick grandpa's voice, something like this: *This is how it was told to me a long time ago. Long ago when the Sun became angry at the people on earth it sent a sickness to destroy them, the Little Men changed a man into a monster snake, which they called Uktena, and sent him to kill her (the Sun). He failed to do the work. Those who know say the Uktena is a great snake, as large around as a tree trunk, with horns on its head, and a bright blazing crest like a diamond on its forehead, and scales glowing like sparks of fire. It has rings or spots of color along its whole length, and cannot be wounded except by shooting in the seventh spot from the head, because under this spot is its heart and its life. The blazing diamond is called Ulun'suti -- "Transparent" -- and he who can win it may become the greatest wonder worker of the tribe. But it is worth a man's life to attempt it, for whoever is seen by the Uktena is so dazed by the bright light that he runs toward the snake instead of trying to escape. Even to see the Uktena asleep is death, not to the hunter himself, but to his family.*

There is another story grandpa told of how one warrior/magician who actually got the diamond and lived. It went something like this: *The Uktena was still asleep, and, putting an arrow to his bow, Âgän-uni'tsï shot senting the arrow through its heart, which was under the seventh spot from the serpent's head. The great snake raised his head, with the diamond in front flashing fire, and came straight at his enemy, but the magician, turning quickly, ran at full speed down the mountain, cleared a circle of fire and the trench he had made earlier with one bound, and lay down on the ground inside.*

The Uktena tried to follow, but the arrow was through his heart.He rolled over in his death struggle, spitting poison down the mountain side. But the poison drops could not pass the circle of fire, it only hissed and sputtered in the blaze, and the magician on the inside was untouched except by one small drop which struck upon his head as he lay close to the ground; but he did not know it.

The blood, too, was poisonous, it poured from the Uktena's wound and down the slope in a dark stream, but it ran into the trench and left the magician 'Unharmed. The dying monster rolled over and over down the mountain, breaking down large trees in its path until it reached the bottom. Then Âgän- uni'tsï called every bird in all the woods to come to the feast, and so many came that when they were done not even the bones were left.

123

After seven days he went by night to the spot. The body and the bones of the snake were gone, all eaten by the birds, but he saw a bright light shining in the darkness, and going over to it he found, resting on a low-hanging branch, where a raven had dropped it, the diamond from the head of the Uktena. He wrapped it up carefully and took it with him. From that time on he became the greatest medicine-man in the whole tribe.

With no one around, tears started rolling down my face as I gripped my M-16 tightly. I cried out loud looking up toward the heavens, "God, damn you why have you forsaken me! If you are up there, please get me home." Then I pointed my weapon in the direction the snake went and emptied my whole clip of ammunition, waking up the entire camp. Everyone thought we were being attacked. Needless to say I got pulled out of the next day's exercises and spent the rest of the time doing pushups with my friend Chief, watching with a big grin across his face. I never knew what that was all about.

The next day it rained even harder. Having met our objectives and accomplished our final task we got orders to pack up and head back in. Even with the rain it just all felt better.

Back in Camp Hansen we lined up in formation waiting to hear what was going to be our next mission. We got rumor that we were going to get a two day R & R but experience has taught me that you just never could tell what was to come next in the

124

good ole Corps. As the Captain marched in front and took command, he went through all the formalities of how good a job we had done in accomplishing our task in the true Marine Corp fashion. There was no other option really. He went on to inform us that indeed we deserved a two day R&R but be ready for another 45 day field exercise upon our return.

He shouldn't have said that because right after his voice screamed "Dismiss", everyone broke out into a mad dash toward the barracks to change and rush out the main camp gate. Just outside the Camp gates was a Japanese town the Marine called the Ville. It is actually in the Genesis book of world records for having the most bars in one general location.

Some Marines were married and had Villa's out in the Ville, surrounding the base camp. Chief had some buddies there inviting him over later for a party. As we sat in one of our favorite bars slamming out some cold ones, he mentioned if I wanted to tag along. Of course I agreed and later that night just as I had forgotten all about everything but bar girls, he rushes in pushing a girl off my lap telling me "Let's go!"

Half way down the street I finally got the words out "Where are we going?" He shouts back "You drunk, to the party!" We walk for a ways down different streets turning here and there. I lose all sense of direction, finally getting to this dirty white concrete apartment building. A beer bottle could be heard bursting on the pavement in the back when screaming voices and Marine yells could be clearly heard calling down for us from above. Looking up we see a bunch of bald heads bobbed up and down to music playing Jim Hendrix. Someone yells down "Chief! Get on up here and have a drink with me, you old Devil Dog."

Just as we got to the door we were met with a big commotion as a bunch of white Marines from another company were leaving or getting kicked out by the sound of it. I heard one say this is bull as he pushed by us going down the stairs.

As we entered everyone quickly forgot about that commotion and started hand shaking and hugging us as a whiskey bottle was shoved into the other hand. We sat down and partied late into the night. Finally everyone started dwindling back toward base camp. Chief and the house owner along with two black Marines and I where the only ones left with a lot of beer.

It was some time late when the front door came bursting in and a bunch of other Marines came rushing toward us. Chief didn't even say a word as he stood and cloths lined the first one in. Flipping that poor Marine off his feet and continuing to rush on towards the open door he cut off the other incoming Marines, giving the rest of us time to join in. It was a good fight for all of us until someone yelled "JP's" (Japanese Police) and that sent everyone off and running.

Out on the street Chief yelled out for me to wait up. As he caught up he bowled over resting on his knees.

"Damn you Okay?" I asked "What was that all about?" "That" he replied "That was fun. Welcome to Okinawa."

We couldn't go back toward base camp because by now our own shore patrol (Military Police) would be looking for us and any drunks to blame this on for Japanese justice. So we headed on down south toward another Japanese town.

We ended up partying on through the next day and on into the night before one of the bar girls mentioned we had better be getting back to base before we go UA (unauthorized absent). This could be bad news for any military person. Depending on the military court hearing, one could be placed on restriction to quarters for 30 days, lose a months pay, lose rank and/or a combination of all three or even get a dishonorable discharge from the military.

Around 2 am the Mama-san said she was closing up and we would have to go. We walked out onto the empty street. Chief says "we're never going to make it back in time." I looked at him, "what do you mean?" He continued saying "there are no more buses running until 7 am". I shouted out loud "What?" He just laughed slapping me on the back "now you will be the same as me, a private!" I looked at him, "Oh hell no I won't." He goes "what the hell are you going to do?" I looked up then down the dark streets and said "I don't know but something."

Just about that time a Japanese man pulled over and

went inside an all night convenient store across the street leaving his car running right in front. I hit Chief in the chest, "Let's go take that car". He laughed again saying "you're stupid". But it was too late I was already running across the street.

I jumped in and tried to get it into gear, but the gears wouldn't work. It didn't help that I had never driven on the right side before. I revved up the engine pushing in the clutch but still no luck. Meanwhile, the Japanese man raced out the store yelling at me at the top of his lungs and started hitting me in the face as I desperately searched to find the right gear. At last I got tired of being pounded in the head and started screaming "Hey! Hey! What the hell!" I jumped out yelling which was enough to frighten the old Japanese man to back up and run to the other side. This gave me just enough time to get back in and finally something in the gear box caught. I scrawled the tires fish tailing the car away, leaving the man tumbling on the pavement.

I got a little ways down the road and saw Chief running out a side street waving his arms like a mad man. We made it back to base camp in time for formation leaving the car on a side street in the Ville. All I can say is Okinawa was a wild place. It wasn't too long after that I rotated back to the states.

One Sunday afternoon everyone started moving around in the Marine barracks from the previous night's parties. Lying around visiting other friends swiping stories someone came up with an idea to find this infamous swimming hole somewhere within the base artillery range. The tale of the luscious swimming hole had been past down from Marine to Marine through this base dating back to the Vietnam War. It was said to be a tranquil place that is hidden away out in the middle of this base, an oasis, with the only fresh water swimming hole on the island. The swimming hole was purposively off limits to enlisted personnel because of the dangers of injuries. Stories of past Marines breaking the rules and ending up severely hurt or dead circulated throughout the base. This is the kind of stuff that intrigues most Marines and temps them to test their own fate. It reminded me of my own childhood upbringing back in the mountains of western North Carolina.

After packing up our rucksacks with beer we headed off in the only direction told in the stories-Northwest of the main gate into the base. We walked the red clay road for as far as we could go. Eventually we had to get off and walk into the jungle terrain for awhile. Finally, we came up to a bridge which we skirted underneath across the steel beams monkey barring and swinging high above a ravine. It took us about two hours of traversing the rough landscape before we found the spot. True to its legend the place was refreshing. There were pools to lounge in and a huge rock face to climb and jump off, a rope to swing off and most importantly shade. It sat down in this deep ravine hidden from all the chaos and heat of the world above.

We had so much fun no one wanted to leave. When

night fall was donning we reluctantly trac back ready to face another day in our hell, back in the good old Marine Corps.

Liberation of Kuwait

Getting back to the United States, it was easy to enjoy the old normal routine way of life. It was also nice to be spoiled by the latest modern conveniences of the states.

It was a beautiful August Friday afternoon at Camp Pendleton, California, and everyone got dismissed around 1630 heading different directions to indulge in their personal free time activities. For most of us single men, this meant barhopping, drinking into oblivion, and trying to chase women. Hanging out on the base enlisted clubs had some advantages like not driving around risking a DUI, but it also ran the high stakes of getting into a bar room brawl. After all, an integral part of being a Marine, taught from boot camp on out, is your duty to help out a fellow Marine in trouble, thus mastering the concept leaving no Marine behind. On base, that duty extended even further by implying your company buddies.

Each individual company has a strong bond generated by having to face difficult situations together. For the Native Americans on base, this was the place we all congregated no matter what company you belonged. Vince had just recently returned from Okinawa, Japan, and a bunch of us were getting together to celebrate. So, on this night we were there looking for trouble. I was leaning up against the dark bar ordering everyone a round of drinks. Suddenly, a message came over the loud speaker announcing a recall for all 1st Marine Divisions to report back to their designated companies. Thinking this was only another "Stand Down," a routine drill, no big deal was expected. It was the Marine Corps discipline to always find a way to mess with your mind. These types of drills would happen quite often to keep us in a state of readiness. So, we kept on drinking, deciding to finish our drinks. That is, until a squad of Marine MP's started walking through the E-club checking ID's. They chased us back to our company area.

Everyone was already standing in formation in front of the company barracks parking lot by the time we arrived. After getting screamed at for being late, we all ran upstairs to change into our camouflage field uniform. Without having a chance to tidy up our rooms or pack up our personal things, we headed back down to the formation with only our field gear. I looked back up at my room feeling as if I was losing my home once again.

After everyone was accounted for, we were marched to the battalion headquarters to fill out paper work. Then, it was on to the armory to check out our weapons.

The main noticeable difference struck me when we were told not to make any phone calls home. Of course, everyone had been keeping up with the news and knew what was going on in the Middle East. So, the first chance anyone got, he dashed off to a pay phone to spread the rumor onto the family. Excitement grew.

It wasn't long before a line of white military buses with dark tinted windows began pulling up in front of our battalion. We started loading up.

After a 20-minute bus ride in the late sleeping hours of the night, reality slowly started to sink-in. Here I was again, looking out a bus window, wondering to myself if this was really happening. The air traffic was really busy at Horton Air Force Base. We were each issued new desert camouflage uniforms, a bandolier loaded with 180 rounds of live M-16 ammo and six highly explosive hand grenades. This changed our mood, reaffirming this was real. We loaded up on C-141 cargo planes that had been pre-loaded with military vehicles.

Twenty-seven long, miserable, cold hours later. The doors opened to the bright flurrying sandy furnace of a heat wave in the Saudi Arabian desert. Looking across the airport tarmac you could just see the heat sizzling off the black pavement. We didn't know at that time this was to be home for the next eight months.

Our first task became apparent as we treked across the runway to our assembly area sporting our new desert camouflage uniforms fully loaded with combat gear and soaked with sticky sweat. Water never tasted so good. We were in no condition to fight at that moment. The sun was brutal.

Since the Saudi government didn't want our presence known to their civilian population, about 30,000 U.S. service men and women were cooped up in warehouses at Bahrain seaport for three seemingly endless weeks. During that time, classes were given, weapons were cleaned and we laid around trying to acclimatize our bodies to the 110 degree desert heat.

One night a terrorist attack occurred without any injuries, but it did shake up enough of the higher-ranking officials to have everyone scattered throughout the desert.

Most of our time was then spent filling a never-ending supply of sandbags. We also built bunkers, refortified gun positions and believe it or not, we exercised. Mail became a personal treasure as well as a day to day venue. It could cheer some up and tear others down, but mail call brought people running like chickens at feeding time.

This was the time I got news from an ex-girl friend that she had accidentally gotten pregnant by a one-night stand. Why she had to write and tell me at this time, I had no idea. This was my equivalent to any Dear John letter. Lucky for me we weren't all, that close at the time, but it hurt just the same. I think it hurt mainly because I guessed she would always be there for me.

Not much action took place between August and January. About the time we would get all settled in, orders would come down for us to move somewhere else. We sent out night patrols to show our presence in an area and on some occasions, received some fleeing fire attacks but sustained no casualties. The sharpness and fine edge on everyone was starting to deteriorate. Reality sank in of an unappreciated world we had taken for granted of back in the States. Life as we knew it seemed like a distant dream. Everyone longed to be with loved ones. Of course, some of us had nothing waiting for us back in the states. I missed my dog.

Finally, on the 1st of February, word came of a date to end our misery. G-day, as it was referred to (ground day), was set for February 15, 1991. A series of events were to take place leading up to that date. On G-1, our unit had a big formation and the commanding officer briefed us on our role in the final phase. We had to write home a last will & testament, this included a statement telling our mothers and fathers that we loved them. Even if, like most of us Native Americans, we had never had to say that kind of stuff to our fathers. They said it could become very important if we did not return. Our parents would always hold it dear. I decided at that moment that whenever I did have children I would always tell them how I loved them.

There were to be two task forces. Task force Ripper would take control of the northern boundaries. Task force Papa Bear would move in from the south. The commanding officer went on to tell us that in this initial push, an estimated 20,000 Marines were expected to become casualties of war. This was no surprise remembering how the boot camp drill instructors where always preaching how we were all expendable. He said he felt privileged to have served with such a fine group of men. If he was trying to lift our spirits up, this was a pathetic attempt to motivate us. We all started plotting a way to kill this incompetent leader. It didn't take long for rumor to get back to him and on the final push he was nowhere to be seen. Our faithful gunny sergeant ended up assuming command.

When G-day arrived we were well on our way by daybreak through our first objective, the minefields that lay along the Kuwait border. There was only slight resistance. The Iraqi POW's became so numerous. That transportation got to be a major problem. Those same Iraqi POW's were practically hanging on to one another desperately trying to leave Kuwait. A lot of them were old men with no fight in them, hungry for some food.

When we did receive fire, it took us all by surprise and gave everyone a lifelong, blood- pumping scare. Some casualties were sustained right away among the chaos. When rounds starting hitting the Amtrak we were riding, they stopped and we disembarked taking up fighting positions around the track; setting up a perimeter as trained. More rounds started hitting the sand making a distinctive snapping sound. It was hard to see who was in control. No one wanted to move.

The gunner on the Amtrak returned some defensive fire. We did the same, not knowing exactly what direction to shoot. Just then, one of the Amtraks made a slight adjustment move to the left and all rounds started firing in that direction.

When it was all over and quietness prevailed once again, radio traffic picked up as someone started announcing, "We're under fire!" This reminded me of a time back home on the "Rez" when our tribal police chief requested backup because he was under gunfire at a house where an Indian witch doctor lived. Dispatch, not fully understanding the radio traffic, sent the fire department. Talk about a funny mistake, everyone on the Rez still laughs about that story. But here, a casualty was being reported and it happened to be a Native American. Word was that one of the Amtraks had ran over a Marine taking cover near one of the tracks when it had to reposition and turn; just an unfortunate mistake.

On another incident, we were tasked with clearing a bunker complex when my fire team came across a large room full of weapons. As we continued to search around the place, I was about to kick open a door when a big explosion went off outside, throwing me against the wall. As we regained our composure and dusted off the sand, I noticed the door was slightly ajar. Slowly opening it I could see a trip-wire device lying on the ground just inside. Word came back over the radio that someone else had just tripped a booby trap with no causalities. With my fire team reassembled behind me, we all opened fire on the door. Afterwards, the remaining door fragments slowly swung partially open. This allowed us to finally kick the door open the rest of the way. Inside facing the door-way, sat a small cannon with the trip wire still connected to the primer laying on the ground. It must have been attached to the door handle waiting for a victim. Luck was on our side that day.

Some incidents I have purposely tried to exclude from my memory. With emotional difficulty, I will now share such painful memories. Our battalion of 1st Marines was supplemented with regiments from the 4th Marines. For a brief moment it was jubilant to see some old buddies that I had gone through boot camp with and even more so to see a childhood, home town buddy. I ran into my good buddy Vince, or, Vinny as he was now known by his fellow Marines. With the casualties we were sustaining, I feared for Vinny's safety and could hardly rejoice at this chance encounter.

The Incident

Pushing farther along we came upon brief resistance, only to be mobbed once again with old Iraqis. Since the battalion was held up awaiting orders on how we were going to transport these POWs back to the rear, our new company commander thought this would be a good time to send a platoon into this newly fortified bunker complex to check for documents.

Since my platoon was 1st platoon, the commander

simply picked us for this task. We needed a couple of radio-men to accompany us. Vinny got designated to go with us and there was nothing I could say to stop this. I just shook my head. He took notice and came up to me to say "What the hell's wrong with you?" I really didn't know except to say, "Just watch yourself, this isn't Boy Scout camp." I got this funny feeling walking up to these positions. I couldn't explain it. The hair on back of my neck was tingling.

The rest of the battalion took up gun positions to cover us. Getting to the spot of the first set of trenches, I jumped in. As my partner followed right behind, sand came caving in after us. Out of sight, we were now on our own. I inched my way forward slowly feeling the ground for any signs of trip wires or booby traps. My partner kept running into my back to the point where I got mad, stopped, turned around holding my bayonet up to his big white eyes and whispered, "Back the fuck off some." He quickly got the message. Going for some distance, we finally came upon a small bunker door. On my hands and knees I pulled myself up close to the bottom of the door and listened.

Satisfied there were no occupants, I hand signaled to my fire team that I wanted my partner to cover me as I was going in. Turning the knob of the door handle, I slowly opened the door with no problem.

Somewhere over in another trench, I could hear the other fire teams going through more bunkers. Some small weapons fire could be heard in the distance.

Once in, I did the same checks and moved on towards a desk. The other Marines were following me in and fanning out to check the corners. It was dark because our eyes hadn't adjusted from the bright outside light. I crawled on around the desk and found a metal bunk bed. Feeling around underneath, I felt a huge wooden box. Feeling on top, my hand came across something. I grabbed a hold of something cold and round. It made me jump and pull my hand away as if I got burned by fire. Dropping the object, I could only watch as it bounced off the ground and rolled toward the back of the bed. My partner yelled out, "grenade!" This started a chain reaction as we all leaped out the doorway pushing each other to the ground. After a few moments with nothing happening, we stood up and resumed our search. Only this time, we walked in letting our guard down, not expecting anything.

I started checking the desk drawers when Vinny decided to open the closet door. Not expecting to find anything in there, he kicked the door open. Within a microsecond a rat-tat-tat noise filled the room, knocking Vinny backward into my back, pushing me over the side of the desk. My M-16 went sailing toward the doorway as I slid off the desk and hit the ground on the other side. My fellow Marines quickly jumped for cover back out the door. Just as I was about to get to my hands and knees, I could see from the corner of my eye more muzzle flashes and someone racing toward the door opening, firing more rounds. He didn't see me. All of his rage was focused on escaping out the open door.

As my own rage kicked in, I leapt forward with all the energy and force I could muster pushing off the floor. I screamed out loud as I hit him just below the armpits somewhere wrapping and locking my arms around him as we both crashed into the wall of sandbags next to the doorway. The thunderous whipping of bullets filled the room about me. My fire team was hunkered down outside. It would be a test of the fittest between me and this bastard who had just shot my best friend. There would be only one sure victor.

It brought memories of the many reservation brawls I had readily engaged in growing up. Part of it had to be contributed to the Marines hand to hand training as well. I had the element of surprise as taught. But, as fast as things were developing, I don't really remember what I was truly thinking at that moment. I was acting on reflexes. As I smashed into this skinny guy, at some point I reached for my bayonet in its sheath on my right side. He clawed at my face as each blow found its mark on his body. I kept hitting my mark until gradually I noticed his strength start to fade. I continued thrusting the blade in as this sticky, wet, warm substance started to cover me. Exhaustion overcame me when my fellow Marines made it into the room yelling, "Stop. He's dead." I simply fell over the lifeless form balled up in the floor.

As fast as it began, it was over. I started yelling, "Dumb, dumb, dumb!" With that, I turned my attention to Vinny who had been hit three times in the chest. He was still alive sucking air through his chest. I just broke down saying over and over, "Oh God, Oh God! You hang in there man. Hang on. Help is on the way." His only words were, "Glad you were here, Dog. I'll see you back home."

With all the rage in me as the Marines looked on, I stood up looking down at this enemy who tried to kill my friends and me. For some unknown reason, like many untold events in war, I reached down as a final act, grabbed the dead soldier by the hair. I picked his head up off the floor just enough to get my knife under his neck and blooded him like a deer back home.

Suppressing my feelings in front of my fellow Marines, I related part of a speech I remembered from a football coach spilled out at a championship game. I repeated something like this, "Listen up! It all comes down to today men. We all have choices now, either we heal as a team or we are going to crumble inch by inch, till we are finished. We can stay here feeling sorely for ourselves and get the shit kicked out of us or, we can stand and fight, one inch at a time."

"The older a person gets, it seems the more things are taken away; its apart of life I guess. But you only learn this when you start losing. You discover life is a game played in inches. Whether it's the game of life like football, the margin for error is so small. One half-a-step too late or too early, you don't quite make it. One half second too slow, too fast, you don't quite get it. The difference is on this team we fight for that inch. On this team we shred to pieces everyone around us, for that inch. We claw our fingernails to the bone for that inch. Because when we add up all those inches, it's going to make the difference between winning and losing, between living and dying."

I continued, "In any fight, it's the guy who is willing to die that's going to win that inch. I know if I'm going to live life anymore. It's because I am still willing to fight and die for that inch, because that's what living is; it's the six inches in front of your face. I can't make you do it. You've got to look at the guy next to you. Look into his eyes. Now, I think you are going to see a guy who will go that inch with you. You're going to see a guy, who will sacrifice himself for this team because he knows when it comes down to it you're going to do the same for him. Now! What are we going to do?"

With that, everyone gave a loud "Hoo-rah," but at the very back someone whispered "play ball!" As always you could always count on someone being a wise guy. We all laughed then loaded up and continued moving forward, leaving Vince for the navy corpsmen to attend. That would be the last I would see of Vinny. The guilt would compress inside of me for many years to come.

From that point on, a vendetta boiled up inside of me. I started liking death. I would take pictures along side

142

the road of dead Iraqi soldiers hanging out of their blown up tanks; their bodies burnt to a crisp. The smell of burnt flesh will forever be embedded in my suppressed memory bank like the smell of boiled shrimp or any other sea food.

The main objective was to take control of the Kuwait International Airport. That was supposed to have taken four to five days of intense fighting. Instead, within six hours we were on that site. Finally, the adrenaline subsided, causing me to fall into a deep depression. I had to get away by myself so I went and sat down in the white, hot sand some distance away by myself. For all the might in the world I could not bring myself to cry. Picking up sand and letting it run through my fingers, I started thinking about death. "Why do I have to live, to kill?"

As a warrior in the old days I would have been expected to kill as a way to provide for my family. But this wasn't killing for necessity. Here, it seemed as if I had killed a friend. For Native Americans there is a connection of all things to the natural elements of the world around us. We call this connection the sacred hoop. When ever a sickness or ailment affects us, we have medicine men that correct our balance with the natural elements of the universe, but I didn't know at the time if there was a cure for meddling on the dark side I was now treading. I now know the other side that few can comprehend. I now have an added responsibility to always have control over the evil that has manifested inside of me, knowing it will always be there to the day I die. The warrior spirit? A true devil dog! Exhaustion over powered me as I fell asleep.

No more to do or mess up, a few days later we finally got the wonderful belated order to pack up and get ready to head home. Sitting on our gear waiting for the freedom bird, I got re-acquainted with my old boot-camp buddy, Iceman from Alaska. We talked about things we wanted to do when our enlistment ended. It was a good sign of another season donning.

Homeward Bound

The plane ride was the most comfortable, long flight back to the States one could hope for. Almost first class, on a commercial flight tailored to fit our every need, well, almost. If you think keeping control of a bus load of elementary kids is hard try a plane load of women starved men who have survived a war. Everyone was talking about what will be the first thing to do when arriving back in the states. One of the few things all Marines could agree on was sex and beer. On the final approach back in the States a loud cheer erupted inside the plane as the airline stewardess announced our arrival back to the United States of America. The true meaning of God Bless America came to mind. A long awaited welcome home climaxed at last, parades, speeches and more parades. I remember walking off the plane on that day and feeling compelled to bend down and kiss the ground promising never again to leave the USA-my homeland.

Part III
Family Ties

Meanwhile back at the Retirement Party John-John keeps searching for the right words to say. He wants to desperately say something that would make a lasting impression on the younger firefighters. Something that they all could relate too, some wisdom that may save their life. But all he could come up with was this reacurring thought of family. Not his own but someone else's. He looks over at his wife whom he fines talking away with another wife and laughing at the momentary pause. He starts reminscining about what Obadi had told him of his struggles with relationships.

The setting is at the front porch of an old run down log cabin, set to the right side facing the yard cluttered with junk and a broken down older car on blocks. The entrance way is gained by two or three wooden steps leading up to the open wood post porch.

A relatively recent addition to the house and running its full width, the porch lacks congruence. It is a sturdy porch with a flat roof. Two wooden chairs sit at one end where a window opens onto the porch.

The yard is a small dirt yard, partially fenced off to the left, with a pile of fire wood, and other farm equipment set off to the side. An old wide oak tree sits idled to the left side with a tire swing hanging helplessly. A wooden hoop with the four native sacred colors of the four directions painted on it lays forgotten among the scattered trash in the yard. A radio sits in the window sill blaring news of anti-war demonstrations and speeches of protest of the countries involvement in the war.

On the isolated reservation all these current affairs seem far off in another time and place as if it hadn't moved on since the Vietnam War of thirty some odd years past. But the impact could be felt just the same as daily radio news announces another home town boy being kill in action. Families mourned and carried out the ritual funnels while others cry and prepare to send another young soul off to join in the countries fight. The difference here is families on this remote reservation have been doing this kind of thing for centuries, and carry on as if it was a tribal duty. For these boys, it was a time to prove themselves worthy, giving a sense of becoming warriors in this modern new world.

In these changing of times as teenage boys come back as aged men, they find themselves in an unrelenting world of confusion, ashamed and often with a broken spirit. Only in the confines of one's culture surrounded by the strength of true loved one's and understanding was there hope for healing and breaking into worlds within worlds, cycle within cycles, and circles within circles, restoring the broken spirit and reaching a true understanding of ones self. This is Obadi's cycle of seasons after hitting the very bottom of his existence. It is said that behavioral change can occur only after one has reached his limit of tolerances, only then can he recognize that he has the power to choose a different course of actions in behaviors. This is why the old ones always said that we all must experience the bad times in order to appreciate the good or we would never know the good we had until it's gone. That's why we have stories.

The Beginning

Sitting slump in a chair on the porch Obadi is in deep sleep, listening to the radio, with a can of beer dangling in his arm. A big monstrous man in his 30's with the look of someone who had endured a lot of stress. Several years had passed since being discharged from the USMC with full honors, a chest full of commendations only to come back to an unwelcoming home, this created a depressed state of mind.

So he just sits and drinks what little pension the military sends him for disability.

Some neighboring kids play war games like the ones he himself once played at their innocent age.

His only life long home town friend who hadn't moved on or away from the rez, he was another veteran. Nicknamed June-Bug, he had served in the Navy. He enters through the fence gate and tries to scatter the kids like walking through chickens in his yard. He tries not to startle Obadi awake, whom he sees napping on the porch. In a round about way

June-Bug comes up and sits on the steps quietly for a spell before engaging in a conversation with Obadi, all the while looking and hoping for a beer like the one dangling in Obadi's hand.

June-Bug wipes his head thinking of some kind of ice breaker to say and finally starts by saying "Hell of a day?" Suddenly wishing he hadn't chosen that particular phrase but it was too late. Obadi quickly snaps up-right in his chair and blurts out "Hell of a day to you? You no good piece of nut skin." Knowing this was coming June-Bug griminess his shoulders looking out at the kids saying "Now why you have to be that way, you know I'm the only one that you can't scare off. Obadi starts to see where this is all leading up to, but continues, "Oh quit your wining! It's the truth ain't it? Besides you only come around when you know I have money. Like everyone else who wants a handout. Where are they when you really need them? Isn't it funny how no-one knows you when you are down at the bottom? Ain't it?

Seizing the moment June-Bug quickly replies "Well that you brought it up. Can I borrow a few dollars? I need a pack of smokes and, or a beer would be nice." Obadi snaps back, "Hell No! Get your lazy ass to work you no good for nothing bum". Then continues asking, "Why would, anyone put up with all this bull when they could easily choose not to". Feeling a little remorse and trying to change the subject he yells into the house for his wife Annie Bee to bring June-Bug a beer or "this loser" as he stated it. Throwing a rock into a plastic who-la-hoop on the ground in front of

148

him June-Bug snaps his figure and balls his fist up bringing it into his chest saying "Now you're talking bro. And, and, just for the record I am your friend Obadi. Remember before the war growing up? I am the only one still here today as your friend. I don't care what other people may say". With this he stops and looks directly at Obadi as if to say "Oops!"

Annie Bee comes out of the house wearing worn-out blue jeans with holes in the knees and a worn white short sleeve shirt. Holding the open can of beer she gives it to Obadi first as he motions with his head toward June-Bug. She gives June-Bug a discusting look but hands him the can.

Watching all this Obadi shakes his head and looks out towards the yard and beyond continuing "Yeah, you're like one of those little puppy dogs looking for momma's tit. Soft, cute and weak! I'll never be like that… This didn't slow June-Bug a bit as he bounced right back "Never say Never! Remember? Getting up out of his chair Obadi stands and holds his can up but stops as he retorts "All those military sayings don't mean-A-God-damn-thing out here in the real world-fool.

Changing the subject June-Bug throws another rock in the yard and asks Obadi, "Why does Annie Bee act, as if she hates me?" He continues saying she used to be the hottest "babe" in high school. "The One!" Obadi simply stated "uh huh, so did my mom before she died". With a big swig of beer he continue telling, how they had not talked to each other real well since he had lost his job a couple of months back. Changing the subject again June-Bug asks Obadi if he remembers playing war games like the kids that where running around in the yard. He states "we never thought we would be running for our life for real. Huh?" This was Obadi's chance to set June-Bug straight when he thought he could be on Obadi's level of thinking. Obadi turns towards June-Bug and said in a matter of fact manner "see that's the difference between you and me. Marines never run, leaving one of our own behind, we stand and fight." June-Bug dropped it by replying, "you know what I mean" Obadi didn't even bother pursuing it any further as well saying, "Yeah I guess, I still run in my dreams. I don't even sleep-good at night any more. You don't understand that". June-Bug sat quiet for only a second until he answered, "Well maybe I didn't experience all that but I was over there". Obadi was getting tired of this conversation and finished off his beer saying "Yeah, I guess, I only wish you would shut up and listen. Listen to the wind." Only June-Bug wasn't missing a beat butting back in "Like you? What do you think of sitting out here on the porch all these days? You know people say you're probably crazy."

Sitting back down into his chair Obadi huffs out "I don't really care what people out there say about me any more, it's what my own people say that worries me. I only care about people in my world. I sit here and I try to see into the next dimension like what our forefathers talked about in our creation stories. Have you forgotten like so many others? Are you so wrapped up into this material world you are ashamed to be called an Indian?"

"There was a time when it felt really proud to be called Indian. Now look around everyone wants to be like everyone else-a non Indian. I just don't care to be around those kinds of people any more. I am who I am." Obadi throws his empty can out into the yard then looks at it for a moment before turning to go into the house. Yelling out "Want another?"

June-Bug shakes his head in agreement as he looks off into the distances thinking at last he murmurs out an "Hmmm!" Just as Obadi hands June-Bug one of the two beers in his hands, he is stop short as a big ruckus erupts out in the yard. In the foreground a kid accidentally gets hit in the arm by another kid with a stick and starts to cry. Obadi starts to open the beer but stops and gets up out of his chair, walks to the edge of the porch and screams out "Knock that crying crap out right now before I come out there and give you all something to really cry about. Cry babies. Men don't cry. Get out of here. Go to your real dads if you can find him around anywhere!" June-Bug takes a big sip of beer shaking his head mumbling "Ohhh Man…" Obadi quickly looks down at him. Standing over him Obadi goes on "What? You loser, Where is your daddy? Right! And there was no one around us to cry to in battle when we lost our friends and brothers in arms. Huh?" June-Bug cowards toward the porch post by the steps as he slips out "Here we go again." Obadi walks back to his chair as he continues "These people that talk, they will never know what it was like over there. Oh but they sure can point a figure and say look how crazy he is. They will never know. But for us that had to endure it, the whole world looks different damn it. What are we suppose to do? What?"

The kid with the injured arm races past Obadi into the house holding his arm sniffling and desperately trying not to cry out loud as he goes by Obadi. It wasn't but a few moments until Annie Bee bursts open the screen door and stops short of Obadi's chair. Obadi bends down, retrieving his beer and finally says "What?" This was Annie Bee's cue as she pleads "Obadi, he could be hurt bad! Why do you have to be like this?" Obadi takes a big swig of beer and replies "Live and learn, they have got to learn sooner or later no one cares about their pain. Nobody wants to hear it. Only the strong survive."

Annie Bee was use to hearing this kind of attitude. Remaining calm she simply states "They're Kids! Family! For Christ's sakes, have you gone and lost your mind along with that heart and soul. These boys sat in church every Sunday to pray for your safe return not their own dads but you. This is how you repay them?"

Annoyed with her being right Obadi finishes off his beer and throws it down by his chair yelling back at her "Aaaah Hell, first of all you talk about fathers-I never had one. Second of all "woman", you mentioned family. Where were they when I really needed them and where are they now? Thirdly

152

"woman", keep that Christianity crap out of my life I am Indian.

Trying to get a hold of the situation he looks down at June-Bug who is watching all this intently he says "Women! Now that's one I can't understand. They always think they are right. I'm going over to Red's bar. Getting out of here! Coming?" As he jumps off the porch and starts walking out of the yard, June-Bug follows along.

Annie Bee continues by saying "Go ahead and run away; just the way you do all your problems. It's so easy for a man; a man, like you. And don't put down my beliefs, at least I have one. You're such an Indian. Real warriors never had all these war problems. Know why? Because those warriors of old had spirituality! A strong spirituality!" Obadi yells back "Shut up woman!" Annie Bee goes on but by this time Obadi and June-Bug, are well out of sight, "Yeah, Women! Man has needed a woman from the beginning of time to always pick him back up when he has failed. It's in the bible." With that she goes back into the house to attend to the injured kid.

Exiting

As Annie Bee starts to examine the young boy she is relieved not to find any open wounds, however she notices a knot forming on the boy's left forearm along with some bruising.

153

With all the stress that has been generated by the argument between her and Obadi, she starts to cry. The young boy sees this and even with all the hurt in him, he feels compelled to try and comfort her instead. So as she puts her head down sobbing into her own hands he automatically starts combing through her long dark hair. After a few moments Annie Bee looks up and wipes her tears off her cheek saying, "It's alright Toby. I'm sorry."

Some of the other kids have come to the door-way and are peeking in as she gets up and walks in a circle, thinking. Finally she stops and looks at the door way then pointing towards one of the bystanders commands, "Syluss go over to Ramsey's house and ask if he can take us to the hospital. Lets see, mom and dad won't be home until after dark. We'll try to call them from town to pick us up. It will be alright.

Syluss steps on into the doorway protesting, "But aunty?" Annie Bee continues commanding, "GO!" as she puts one hand on her hip and the other she points in the direction for the bigger kid to go. So he turns and disappears around the house lazily trotting off, lowering his head he mumbles "God, I do everything around here". Toby who is now resting on the couch lies down holding his injured arm over his stomach. He looks up at Bee and says, "Aunty? Why doesn't he like us kids? Puckering his lips out toward the doorway he throws his head upward and outward making a pointing gesture mimicking the same gesture Obadi adopted from one of the western powwows that he had dance at, but that's another story.

This takes Annie Bee by surprise as she realizes how the argument between her and Obadi could affect her own kids as well. She starts "He does! He just doesn't want to show it anymore. See, time and circumstances changes a person." She takes up a seat next to him putting his head in her lap before continuing, "Sometimes I think he is truly lost in this world and has no one to ask for direction. He doesn't have a dad like he is to you all. He has learned to survive by becoming this certain kind of mean and tough person without the weaknesses of feeling any emotions to the point that he becomes that mean person. I know he doesn't like who he has become. You've had to have known him before he went off to the war. He was so cute and innocent. He was fun to be around. A string of Annie Bee's hair dangles onto Toby's face as he plays with it she continues, "In the old days the Old ones had a special ceremony for the warriors coming back from battle. No-one hardly does that ceremony any more. I think that's what is missing now days with our young men coming back. There's no release from that bad spirit."

Toby is about to fall off to sleep when a car engine is heard outside pulling up behind the house. It stops and two car doors are heard being slam shut. Syluss appears in the door with a tall cowboy wearing the wrangler jeans and jacket topped with a black cowboy hat. This would be Ramsey, Annie Bee's ex-boyfriend from high school days. He speaks first saying, "Well, dear. What have you gotten yourself into this time?" Annie Bee gets up off the couch stating, "Please, not now, my boy got his arm badly injured. We need to get him to the hospital. No one's around and well I need some assistances, please."

Ramsey steps on in taking his Cowboy hat off surveying the house before looking at the kid as he blurts out, "Where's that no good, big shot Ram-Bow friend of yours. Gone batty again or just locked up?" Annie Bee is in no mood to play word games with another macho man so she puts both hands on her hips and in a soft monotone voice says, "Look, are you going to help or not?" Ramsey shrugs his shoulders answering "You know I am always here for you sweety!" Not missing a beat Annie Bee turns to get the boy ready huffing, "Maybe for any other violable woman. Not this woman!" Ramsey fires back, "Ain't we all? Come on, didn't we have a good thing going at one time?" Annie Bee stands up and turns to face him with the boy in her tiny arms, she starts demanding, "You messed that up, sleeping with that whore. Now I have gotten on with my life and found a man who used to show me real Love, as a "Person" not just for my body. Are you going to help? If so can we please go!" Not wanting to push this conversation any further Ramsey simple says, "Hey, why sure… Let's!" Annie Bee turns her attention to Toby reassuring him by whispering, "It'll be alright." She looks at Syluss who has been watching intently from the door, "Syluss go inside and get my purse. Hurry!" They slowly depart around the house and get into the car then head on into town.

She Devil

A moon full in its grander lights up the dark mountainous landscape and cast dark shadows among evil beings that ventures around these woods preying on any gullible soul. The Cherokees have stories of similar beings referred to as "The Little People". They play games on people wondering through the woods alone. These are invisible people only to be seen by people of troubled minds. They are said to have long black hair and look like Indians. Some say they dwell in the rocks or Laurel thickets and have been known to have stolen away loud misbehaving Indian kids. These kids are never to be seen again. This was what Obadi and June-Bug were discussing as they stagger back from the local bar. Making jokes about tonight's unfortunate foil, the people being arrested at the bar fight they have just fled from. Sadly those people will not be sharing this spirited moment. However, Obadi and June-Bug knew if they, themselves where in that situation they would want the party to continue. Not a care in the world. It is good to be at home in the woods. That is until they round the house and stumble up the steps to find themselves locked out. Obadi fumbles around for a second into his pocket dropping his beer he was carrying and stops. He slams a fist into the wooden door, screaming, "Why? Why she gotta do this?"

June-Bug pops up onto the porch saying, "Ah well, we still have this…" trying to keep the atmosphere, spirited. This caught Obadi by surprise as he saw the beer in June-Bugs hand. He quickly answers "Hell yeah! Think you sir, may I have another." June-Bug didn't want to lose the positive mood so he quickly relies, "Damn right, Jar-Head!" This really ticks off Obadi going back to the Marine days screaming out, "Speak up when you address me Squid". The remark got under June-Bugs skin so after a long swig of beer he changed the subject, "Hey, look at the full moon! Wonder what kind of trouble will happen tonight?" A long pause falls on the two as they glare up at the brightness of the moon. June-Bug finally breaks the silence with, "Haven't ever seen anything more beautiful in life than this". Obadi pops open a beer as he relates, "Man, nobody looks up at the sky, the moon, the stars now a-days." June-Bug answers, "Yeah, remember how beautiful and peaceful it would seem during the war? Obadi starts reminiscing whispering, "Yeah…" then after a second thought he caught on to June-Bugs game saying, "Shut up! Where I was at, it was murderous looking. You always knew someone was going to get hit tonight because if you can see them, they see you." June-Bug paid no attention saying, "Just saying! You know we had to have something that we found peace in. That's all I'm trying to say."

After a long pause Obadi takes a long swig of beer and starts, "Okay, mud for brains, for me? Yes, I found my peace in that group of stars. It was at a time when everything seemed upside down. I would look up at that certain group of stars that form a backward seven. No one to turn to for the right answers and no one cared but I got my strength to carry on by praying to the heavens, that certain group of stars, but it didn't change a thing. It didn't protect my friends. Bleeding to death in my arms, watching death flood out the remaining life in their eyes knowing all time is stopping for them. I know you can't understand. You were on a damn boat. I know you don't feel guilty but I do. I've lost something over there. I feel empty as if I shouldn't be here today. I have nothing..." He sits down in his chair as June-Bug tosses his can in the yard. In the foreground Obadi sees a shadow by the tree but as soon as he tenses up a soft voice catches June-Bugs ear as he turns his good ear where the soft powwow - 49 singing can be heard. As he rolls his eyes up towards Obadi he motions, "Now that's sounds like the devil." Obadi slaps June-Bug in the back whispering, "Hey, Shhhh... a she devil..." June-Bug continued, "you're messing with fire..."

Out from among the tree strolls a tiny figure wearing the tightest cowgirl jeans with the hip to match that magnificent swing announcing in a soft voice," Why? It's true." Obadi getting brave steps forward proclaims, "What's true? Baby!" The figure steps more into the moonlight introducing herself, "It's me Obadi, remember me? Candy...Remember that night? I knew you long before all this." As she spins around on the pole onto the porch saying, 'Now here we are again."

On this note either June-Bug sensing three was a crowd or he just didn't want to stick around to see how Annie Bee was going to take all this, says his good-byes and leaves.

Obadi gets up from his chair getting a little closer to
Candy before beginning, "Have a beer." As he hands
her a can he looks at her up and down continuing,
"It's good to see you again, Damn it's been a long
time." Candy replies, "Yeah, I heard you guys
hooping it up at the bar. It was only a matter of time
before trouble started. I said to myself "hey if he lives
through this mess, I want that Indian man tonight for
myself. Know what I mean?" Obadi takes a big drink
of his beer as he blurts out, "I guess you heard I got a
woman?" She nods with, "Of course, Bee is a
distance cousin of my... I hardly knew her, I grew up
in California. Anyway aren't we all related one-way
or another on this rez?" In agreement Obadi retorts,
"Hell yeah, now that is the truth. Grandma was
always saying you can't be with so and so because
that's your cousin on so and so side." Candy laughs
as she looked around saying, "So where is she
anyway? I wouldn't leave my man out in the cold,
alone in the full moon light. A lover's moon for sure."
Obadi takes up a seat on the steps as he raises both
arms saying, "Hell, I don't know. Locked out though,
maybe she had enough of me and left." Candy sits
down beside him putting her head on his shoulder
saying, "Poor thing, anything I can do to help out?
We could talk or just listen to the night go by. Obadi
puts his head on her and says this is perfect. He starts
to remember his younger days when his grandpa use
to tell old Cherokee stories. He looks up at the sky as
Candy keeps talking saying "Have you heard this
one: *Long ago when the world was young, there
were not many stars in the sky. In those days the
people depended on corn for their food. Dried corn*

160

was made into corn meal by placing it inside a large hollowed stump and pounding it with a long wooden pestle. Then the cornmeal was stored in large baskets. During the winter, the ground meal could be made into bread and mush. One morning an old man and his wife went to their storage basket for some cornmeal. They discovered that someone or something had gotten into the cornmeal during the night. This upset them very much for no one in a Cherokee village stole from someone else. Then they noticed that the cornmeal was scattered over the ground. In the middle of the spilt meal were giant dog prints. These dog prints were so large that the elderly couple knew this was no ordinary dog. They immediately alerted the village. It was decided that this must be a spirit dog from another world. The people did not want the spirit dog coming to their village. They decided to get rid of the dog by frightening it so bad it would never return. They gathered their drums and turtle shell rattles and later that night they hid around the area where the cornmeal was kept. Late into the night they heard a whirring sound like many bird wings. They look up to see the form of a giant dog swooping down from the sky. It landed near the basket and then began to eat great mouthfuls of cornmeal. Suddenly the people jumped up beating and shaking their noise makers. The noise was so loud it sounded like thunder. The giant dog turned and began to run down the path. The people chased after him making the loudest noises they could. It ran to the top of a mountain and leaped into the sky, the cornmeal spilling out the sides of its mouth. The giant dog ran

161

across the black night sky until it disappeared from sight. But the cornmeal that had spilled from its mouth made a path way across the sky. Each grain of cornmeal became a star. The Cherokees call that pattern of stars, "the place where the dog ran."

As she finishes up the story and looks, Obadi is fast asleep.

Caught In the Act

Obadi didn't know if he passed out or simply went to sleep on Candy that night. One thing was certain it was morning and the sun was cresting the horizon when Annie Bee bounces onto the porch. Startled Obadi jumps up; looks around as if he had lost something. Annie Bee continues unlocking the door saying, "Oh you, you scared me!" Obadi sits up in his chair as he rubs his aching head. He hears a car pulling away. He yells out, "Who the hell was that?" Annie Bee opens the door and as she steps in she stops momentarly to say, "Who? What? Oh that?" Pointing with her free hand she goes about her business trying to avoid Obadi's confrontation saying "that was nobody." Obadi gets up and chases after her protesting, "Don't lie, who was that?" Annie Bee gets to the kitchen table and stops, turning around she huffs, "Obadi, don't do this." This only makes Obadi even more mad as he pushes on asking," Who was that you whore. Are you messing around on me?" Annie Bee turns around facing the sink claiming, "Nooo… Don't say that!" Obadi walks around to face

162

her contesting, "Then, Tell me!" Annie Bee walks away saying, "It was nobody! Just... you..." Obadi yells out, "damn you, you went back to that low life piece of dirt cowboy, didn't you?" Annie Bee trying desperately not to provoke this any further answered, "Nooo... I love you." But Obadi was in no mood to hear this, shouted, "Shut up! How can you say that? You don't even know how to love. You bitch." He walks out side slamming the door but stops at the edge of the porch just as Annie Bee comes out saying in a calm voice, "I love you Obadi, don't do this. We took Toby to the clinic and I stayed over at Mom and Dad's until they could bring me back this morning. Why are you doing this?" By now Obadi had to save face so he continue asking, "Okay, if you love me? I mean really love me... Prove it!" Annie Bee fires back, "What? I'll do anything for you!" Obadi still not trusting her turns to her and commands, "Alright, if you really love me then throw away all those damn pictures of him you have stashed away in those boxes in your closet." Annie Bee suddenly breaks into a little laugh but it quickly subsides into anger as she says, "Why? You're jealous? Obadi yells back, "I'm not jealous, I just want to see if you will do this." Annie Bee can't believe this proclaiming, "No... They're just pictures..." only to have Obadi continue, "Well, just throw them away. Better yet let me see you burn them." Annie Bee tries to walk away saying "NO!" and shuts the door. Obadi grabs her by the shoulders and twirls her around forcefully. Annie Bee feeling put out with his behavior slaps Obadi across the face. Obadi then tries to reach for a second time spitting out angrily "Why you whore!" This time she punches Obadi square in the nose making it bleed. This enrages Obadi seeing his own blood, cursing mad he recoils from the punch and back hands Annie Bee across the face saying "Oh you want to act like a big bad bitch, I'll treat you like one!" This slap sent Annie Bee flying over the living room couch crying, as she quickly covers her face. Feeling guilty, Obadi rushes over saying "Oh I'm sorry babe!" Annie Bee turns over facing the back of the couch and says "Just leave." Obadi yells out, "well fine! I'm out of here, this isn't my place anyway, you don't love me" as he kicks the door open he walks through the yard kicking the hoop and some beer cans.

It's an Indian Thing

Several weeks have gone by since the break-up. Annie Bee finds herself in a depressed state laying around on the couch, crying. Then one day Candy comes knocking on the door of Annie Bee's house. Annie Bee opens the door in her p.j's as Candy smiles and says, "My goodness, look at you cuss", seeing the black eye she continues, "got you some real Indian love?" Annie Bee answers "I thought that was when a girl got a black eye and a hicky on her neck". Candy hugs her saying "well you're half way there who knows when he comes back?" Annie Bee pulls back retorting "Hope he dies!" Candy is caught by surprise changing the subject she goes "Mom sent me over to check on you. Are you alright? Is there anything I can do?" Confused, Annie Bee, tries to hind her eyes from the brightness of the clear sky saying, "I'm alright, I don't know something is going on with him and I don't know if I even care anymore. Come on in." She turns and flops back onto the couch as Candy pulls up a chair from the kitchen saying, "Hush, that kind of talk. It feels bad now and probably it will always be there but we Indian women must stick together, be strong and you see we will carry on, it's tradition. Grandma said *"During the Cherokee removal to the West called, "the trail of tears", was said too be a long and treacherous journey and many were dying along the way. The Elders knew that the survival of the children depended upon the strength of family that only the women could carry. One evening around the campfire, the Elders called upon Heaven Dweller, (ga lv la di). They told Him of the People's suffering and tears. They were afraid the children would not survive in this new world. Gal v la di e hi spoke to them, "To let you know how much I care, I will give you a sign. In the morning, tell the women to look back along the trail. Where their tears have fallen, I will cause to grow a plant that will have seven leaves for the seven clans of the Cherokee. Amidst the plant will be a delicate white rose with five petals. In the center of the blossom will be a pile of gold to remind the Cherokee of the white man's greed for the gold found on the Cherokee homeland. This plant will be sturdy and strong with stickers on all the stems. It will defy anything which tries to destroy it .For this I give to show all one needs is in his own heart and soul." The next morning the Elders told the women to look back down the trail. Sure enough a plant was growing fast and covering the trail where they had walked. As the women watched, blossoms formed and slowly opened. They forgot their sadness. Like the plant the women began to feel strong and beautiful. As the plant protected its blossoms, they knew they would have the courage and determination to protect their children who would always carry the pride of the Nation towards West".*

So you see come on now, we have got to get you up, get busy and pretty soon you'll see it'll get better." Annie Bee sits up but stops to say, "Oh Candy, Thanks but I don't know what I am going to do now. My whole world was centered around him. I just don't know I suppose I could get back to my old routine again….but?" Candy butts in, "Honey, things happen for a reason. We never know why at that moment, but I believe if it's meant to be it will work out in time." This doesn't move Bee a bit instead she replies, "Time? I don't have time. My clock is ticking away fast now. Candy continues, "You'll learn honey, the powers of the universe doesn't work on our time clocks. Everything has its' own time and place."

Annie Bee looks up fixing her hair as she mumbles, "Is this an Indian thing?" Candy let's out a little laugh as she goes on, "An Indian thing? I suppose, it sure use to be. It's around all of us. Everything has its' place-that's what the old one's use to tell us. Remember?" Annie Bee finally gets up and walks toward the kitchen saying, "You make every thing seem so simple and to think you're younger then me."

166

But Candy continues, "Simple? Now, you're catching on, it only seems hard when we get all caught up in this society." Annie Bee pours them both a cup of tea when she states, "Yeah, well make this simple I think I may be carrying Obadi's baby. And to tell you the truth it would just as easy be Ramsey's if only he could, you know. Oh but Obadi is so jealous I can't talk to him. She slides a cup toward the other end of the kitchen counter toward Candy followed by a long silences. Finally Candy breaks in, "Oh my God, dear. What are you planning on doing?" Annie Bee puts the cup down and lowers her head saying, "Why I am going to have it... It's a part of me, and probably the only good thing left in this relationship."

Moment of truth

It's another hot humid day in the southern mountains Obadi is laid out underneath an old oak tree, asleep. When his only acquaintance these days is his old drinking buddy June-Bug stops by for a chat. Announcing his arrival, June-Bug hollers out, "Reveille! Reveille! Reveille!" Obadi jumps up bumping his head on a limb and falling back to the ground saying, "Hooooly, hell man, can't you just leave me alone. Why must you always bug me June-bug?" June-Bug kept on, as he stood over Obadi at the position of attention, "Get up Marine, get up. No one gave you an order to be laying down. Get your sorry ass up and at it." Obadi scoots his back up against the tree as he rubs his head yelling out, "Get out of here and take all that Marine B.S. with you before I beat the crap out of you. Leave!" June-Bug looks at Obadi for a moment then turns to leave. At that time Obadi gets up and dusts himself off saying, "Hey! Man I was just kidding. Come on back here, I have something to ask you."

June-Bug stops and performs a sloppy military turn around refered to as an about-face then he gives up the whole military act as he spits out, "Dude you feeling alright, I've never heard you call anyone back. You always chase people away, but never call someone back. What can I do? Go buy some more beer?" Obadi rubs his head again as he looks out over the landscape saying, "No, man, people do change you know." June-Bug looks at Obadi weird as he relies, "Can they? What's wrong with you? You're talking crazy now." Obadi walks out into the pasture a little as he shouts, "Sure, they can." June-Bug quickly shoots back, "You're saying you are about to change? But man you have always said to me no-one would ever get to the King D.O. double G-dog." Obadi walks back under the comforting shade of the tree to say, "Maybe. You know I laid out here all night just thinking. Thinking what I had, what I had lost and well just wondering what does it all mean. Where am I supposed to go from here? You know when you have it all you don't have to think so hard. I guess at some point a man has got to swallow some proud. Haven't you just had to stop and think? About anything?"

June-Bug sits down with his back resting against the tree looking up at Obadi as he points to himself saying, "That's all I do all the time." Obadi laughs saying, "No, I mean thinking to the point of seeing the truth... I look around at this old oak tree and I became the tree and everything else seemed to evolve around it. It didn't matter what was happening in other places. I saw how things have their own place. You appreciate the beauty of knowing you had the power to manipulate something but yet accepted the choice of letting it be left alone. Then I understood what the old ones used to say about life being about choices. We can find peace within ourselves if we choose too." Obadi lies back down to sleep as June-Bug remains quiet looking up at the clouds passing over in the blue sky.

Burned

During all this time broken-up from Annie Bee, Obadi stay over at some of his drinking buddies. After he straighten up he finally had the nerve to go back to his moms and dads place.

One day he decides to go over to Annie Bee's house to work on the old junk car sitting in the yard. As he tinkers around under the hood of the old car he can be heard talking to himself saying, "Come on Old Faithful, we gotta get you back on your feet now..." This entire disturbance gets the attention of Candy as she comes to the window to see what was going on. Seeing Obadi she steps onto the porch calling out, "Hello, Obadi, It's so good to see you again. What are you doing there?" Startled and bumping his head on the hood Obadi grabs a rag out of his back pants pocket and starts to wipe his hands as he cordially replies, "Ah... Hi! I didn't think anyone was home. Ah well, I thought I would get this piece of junk out on the road again." Candy walks down into the yard closer to Obadi as she quietly states, "To tell the truth, it never bothered me. Actually it seems as much apart of this place as that tree. Reminds you of all the good times it had in its day." Obadi steps back a little gasping, "I guess you're right. That's funny, never thought about that." As he looks around asking, "Where's Bee?" Candy tries to get closer as she tells, "Ohhh, I wouldn't worry about her. She's probably over at that Ramsey's house again. Ah, Ohhh, I'm sorry... Maybe I shouldn't have said anything dare I have such a big mouth."

Disappointed but trying not to show it Obadi goes back to work saying, "It's alright." Candy walks on up to Obadi and puts her arm around him whispering into his ear, "Yeah, well Honey you can always show me some Indian love...." Obadi continues messing around with the car lowering his own head as if in defeat. At this time another car is heard pulling up in the back of the house. A car door shuts and Annie Bee appears around the corner of the house. She instantly sees Obadi and Candy next to the old junker. Putting a little more quick into her step she walks right up to him as he wipes off his hands. In an anger tone she chastises Obadi with, "Oh, you have some nerve showing up at my place again." She looks directly at Candy saying, "And you, what are you trying to do, screw all-my cousin's. Candy turns red in the face as

170

she blurts out, "Oops, I better go back inside."

She tries to skirt by the two but Annie Bee stops her saying, "No, you stay… I want to know what's been going on around here." Obadi raise both arms telling her, "Nothing is going on." But Annie Bee is to streaming mad to settle for this answer and pushes on, "Nothing is going on? Nothing is going on? You never even once bother trying to get this car to run this whole time you've been back from the war. What makes you care now? Obadi pleads, "Look Annie Bee that's why I am here, to tell you I have changed. I quit drinking. I'm sorry I hurt you." Annie Bee starts crying saying, "You can't change, just, go away." Obadi continues pleading, "But, but, Ah Candy! Tell her." Candy feels cornered and sees an opportunity rebounding she says, "What? Deny we all had some good times in this old car." Annie Bee is still crying as she slaps Obadi in the face and yells, "I dare you to Hit me again, I'll have you thrown in jail so long. Uh, I hate you…" as she turns and runs back to the car behind the house which has been waiting with the engine running the whole time. Obadi starts to run after her looking back at Candy saying, "What the hell are you talking about?" Just before he gets to the corner of the house the car can be heard racing away.

On Wings of Eagles

Sitting on the porch in front of Annie Bee and Obadi's old house June-Bug and Obadi watch the boys play cowboy and Indians like when they where

171

young. Hardest part about this game was deciding who was going to be the cowboys because the cowboys always got killed first. No one wanted to be roughed up and killed right away.

Obadi started talking, "Did you here?" He throws a rock in the yard. June-Bug sits in a sober mood looking out at the game going on saying, "Yeah..." Obadi finally breaks a moment of silence asking, "I didn't see you at Annie Bees' funeral?" Another long silence before June-Bug comes back with, "I know I wasn't sure if I should go besides I'm not into that kind of thing." Obadi rocks back and forth in his chair saying, "Wonder why she wouldn't tell me she was pregnant?" June-Bug throws another rock into the yard then says, "I don't know bro, but grandma said that's why Candy moved in with her when you left her." Obadi wonders out loud, "What? Candy knew all this time?" June-Bug doesn't want to get in the middle of another argument and says, "I don't know but people around the rez are saying that Candy has always wanted a kid by you. You know she can't have any kids on her own." After another long silence Obadi stretches his arms toward the sky and in a monotone voice he tells June-Bug his next move, "Hey, June-Bug I heard from the forest service about a fire job. I'm going to take it. I need to get away for a while and think. I need to make some money to provide for these boys." June-Bug fires back in surprise, "you're going to raise Annie-Bee's two boys?" Obadi looks out into the yard saying "I'm all the family they have now. Hell fire their own dads don't want nothing to do with them. They didn't even come the Annie Bee's funnel."

At about this time Candy comes from around the corner of the house carrying a newborn baby. June-Bug gets up and says his ritual "Goodbye" only this time Obadi gets up and gives him a big bear hug saying "you take care, buddy" that was all. That would be the last he would ever see of June-Bug because a few years later June-Bug would be found dead in his trailer. Drunk himself to death they said but in reality it is probably just another uninvestigated murder on the reservation.

Candy sees this as she sits down in Obadi's chair until he turns his attention to her. He walks up to the two in the chair and spills out what he has in mind to do. She doesn't get sad or act surprised only saying, "You do what you think you must do. We'll be here" Obadi walks among the kids playing war and stops to pick up the hoop in the yard. He examines it more closely then tries to dance through it, he stops holds it out and hands it to one of the kids saying, "You'll see, everything works in circles." With this he walks on out of the yard not looking back. He didn't know he was only creating another statistic like the broken family hoop of so many others on the reservation. This was late spring when April showers brought May flowers that Obadi noticed popping up out of the ground along side the road he was traveling west on.

Part IV
Baptism by Fire

Obadis' promise, never to leave the good old USA, is what John-John was thinking about as he tried to finish up his Retirement Party speech. It's funny to notice the traits one takes on with age. For instance there was a time when getting up to speak in-front of a crowd was just too hard to do. I guess it would be because of the risk of exposing yourself, but as you age that doesn't seem so important anymore. And it would be easy to get distracted when something out of the ordinary went hey wire like the glass cup dropping off the podium and everyone getting a big kick out of that at this retirement party. But with experience an old timer/experienced leader of men, will always find a way to take advantage of any given situation. This is one lesson learned from one of my best friends that only he could tell you if he was here. John-John starts reminiscing the passed "I tell you, I learned more about life and fire with him than in any other season since. So I tell it from my perspective after the events:

Day 1
Monday, April 13

My first true induction into this "fire culture" emulated on a gloomy Monday morning. It was out west in the summer of 1993, on a fire in the Jemez Mountains of New Mexico. I had worked a season in the southern region with the Asheville Hotshots before transferring here as the result of some trouble I had encountered on that crew. Here I was working for the Bureau of Indian Affairs (BIA) in the western region. Talk about being treated as an outsider. No one knew anything about me, or my past with this agency. I was placed on a Type 6 model 52 Wildland Fire Engine that supported a 250-gallon water tank, perched atop a 1990 Ford F-10 pickup truck chassis.

In the fire management program, engines are typed according to size, water capacity and pumping capabilities. Type I classifications are given to the largest engines. The smallest is Type 7.

I worked as a seasonal crewmember which is somewhat misleading. The work was actually fulltime for the duration of the fire season, however long that might last. Usually, we could expect to be employed from mid April through September. However, seasonal hires were not entitled to the same benefits as permanent employees. We did not receive retirement and health care benefits, but it was good money for summer work. The fire gig was perfect for college students with a sense of adventure and a longing for the serenity of the great outdoors.

As a rookie on one of my first assignments, I wasn't expected to know a lot. Our crew was made up of three older and more experienced local individuals. We all rode cramped up in the cab of the agency fire engine. We each had predetermined assignments that had been practiced over and over long before we were sent out on an actual fire assignment. For instance, there are a lot of training and physical fitness requirements that must be satisfied prior to the fire season. So, when that first call comes in from dispatch, excitement fills the air. For a rookie, it can be overwhelming, creating even a more dangerous environment. It's a scenario that experienced fire personnel know all too well. That kind of excitement could get you or someone else seriously injured before you even reach the scene of the incident. It's also the kind of excitement that entices firefighters into the career in the first place. Even after years of experience, seasoned firefighters have to remind themselves not to get in too a big rush. Slow down, focus and make sure your instincts are geared towards the situation at hand and the elements surrounding that environment called situational awareness. That is the keen ability to assess and know what is happening around you at all times. Know the weather conditions, fire activity, types of fuels, potential hazards, location of your crew members, where the safety zone and escape routes are, available resources and be aware of changing conditions. The first time out, firefighters tend to overlook situational awareness. You're overwhelmed by the force and mesmerized by its magnitude or just by the sheer excitement of the fire. You just want to see it; the massive wall of flames with its fingers extended out beckoning you to come closer.

As we don our famous bright yellow nomex shirts, the Engine Boss is gathering essential information from our Fire Management Officer (FMO.) He or she is the supervisor and most respected in the fire organization. Everyone knows, in order to reach this level in the fire world, this person has paid their dues. They have spent many years training and experiencing all disciplines of fire management. The FMO relays information like who to report to upon arrival at the incident, the best travel route, current and predicted weather conditions and known hazards. Of course, those are only a few facets of duties from a long list of informational requirements.

We pull the engine out and let it warm up as we make sure we have all of our personal gear and protective equipment on the truck. We check our water supply and radio's not forgetting to stock up on extra batteries and grab our lunches.

By this time, the Engine Boss walks out of the office with all the paperwork. We load up and head out. As we pull out, the Engine Boss turns to the local, experienced hands and says, "This fire is reported in the asbestos zone area; the place no one thought could carry any fire."

En-route, we listen intently to the radio traffic and make mental note of other resources heading in the same direction. As fire personnel arrive on the scene, they start funneling vital information back to dispatch. They report the size of the fire, the best route to get to it, the location of the staging area, and who is going to be in charge; the Incident Commander (IC). They also report what type of structures, if any are in danger. This information will help to determine if air support or other types of resources will be needed.

Exiting the interstate, we see a column of white smoke plume towering high up into the atmosphere, rolling over the Jemez Mountains. The smoke column is a good indicator of the kind of fire activity. A trained eye can observe the smoke column and determine which direction the fire is moving, wind direction, air stability, fire intensity and what stage of involvement the fire is in. Again, it takes a wealth of experience to learn to recognize these things and accurately assess fire behavior. As a rookie, I was in awe at the site of the plume and shocked at the volume of smoke this natural demon was putting up. I kept thinking, "Are we really going to fight this thing?"

Upon arrival at the staging area, all the bosses representing the various resources got together and started formulating a plan of attack. This meeting is called a briefing. For a first timer, the whole ordeal seemed like total chaos. But, I would later learn that a lot of important things are happening all at once in this initial attack plan. As experience will teach you, this can be a very stressful time. There is no need for everyone doing his or her own thing, following a separate sheet of instructions.

As the leaders got briefed and came up with a game plan, the rest of us waited by the engines, visiting with other engine crewmembers. Some were getting reacquainted with old timers or folks they had worked with on previous fire details. The fire world is small in that sense. The friendships you make will be rekindled year after year when you meet on fire details no matter where they are. The fire world is a tight knit community.

Soon, the group disperses and we see our Engine Boss walking towards us with a purpose in his step. He is toting a wad of paper and maps in one hand and his radio in the other.

As he gets closer, he tells the others exactly what their duties will be. He then unrolls his wad of paper on the hood of the truck and starts tracing our current location and our destination. He also ensures that we all know where our safety zones will be in case, God forbid something should go awry. A safety zone is pretty much self-explanatory. It is a safe place we could wait while the fire passes by. It's also imperative to know what escape route we will need to take to get back to that spot.

No one asked any questions so we all jumped back in the Engine, following a parade of vehicles heading up an old logging road. Long before we see flames, we smell smoke. We make our way up to a spot of blackened vegetation along the roadside. Flames are still burning in spots. We pull over, allowing the entourage to pass us by. This was going to be our mission; find the point of origin and start establishing a wet line east along the road until we tie in with another engine tasked with securing the east flank. We hose down the flames, extinguishing all hot spots we find. This was the initial attack phase. It's quick and dirty; the first operational period of a fire. Old policy dictates that all agencies will try to extinguish all fires within the initial attack phase. It was known as the 10 a.m. rule. For nearly a century, agencies followed that concept so well that it has built up an enormous volume of fuel loading in some areas. As a result, fires are becoming more intense causing managers in all departments to re-evaluate policies and consider putting fire back into the ecosystem. Fire is good for the environment. Old Indians have always held that belief. This fire helped others adopt the native concept and implement a change in policy.

The least experienced person on the engine was assigned the duties of hose handler. While the engine boss stayed close to the radio directing the operation, the other guy operated the engine pump and helped pull hose line out. It's important work but not very exciting, being away from the flaming front. Everyone wants to be up closer to the beast at first; not knowing any better.

It must have been sometime after lunch, maybe around 1 p.m. Progress was coming along slowly. From the sound of the radio traffic, we were in for a long haul. It would be an extended attack and possibly a night shift. Since this incident was on BIA land, we were the ones expected to pull the extended shift.

Day 2
Tuesday, April 14

We did as expected and stayed out on the same line for two more days and nights. This was before agencies implemented the work/rest guidelines they adhere to today. We were stuck there until the end. The fire just kept growing. Rumor had it right, on the third day a Type 2 Incident Management Team was coming in to take over.

Incident Management Teams are set up to relieve area command. A type 2 team is usually assigned when it appears the fire will not be contained during initial attack and has the potential to keep growing. When things get too large for the local team to handle, a type 1 management team is called in. Type 1 teams are comprised of experts from all across the nation. This incident would see both before it was over.

Today a hummingbird kept buzzing around us. I figured it thought our yellow shirts might be flowers. The pueblo guys say the hummingbird is a messenger of death, it's the Screech owl for the Cherokee's. What was it trying to tell us? This reminded me of our Cherokee creation stories one of The First Fire. Grandpa told it something like this: *In the beginning there was no fire, and the world was cold, until the Thunders Beings who lived up in Galunlati, (Cherokee word for heaven) sent their lightning down and put fire into the bottom of a hollow sycamore tree which grew on an island. The animals knew it was there, because they could see the smoke rising out at the top, but they could not get to it on account of the water, so they held a council to decide what to do. This was a long time ago.*

Every animal that could fly or swim was anxious to go after the fire. The Raven offered, and because he was so large and strong they thought he could surely do the work, so he was sent first. He flew high and far across the water and lighted on the sycamore tree, but while he was wondering what to do next, the heat had scorched all his feathers black, and he was frightened and came back without the fire. The little Screech-owl volunteered to go, and reached the place safely, but while he was looking down into the hollow tree a blast of hot air came up and nearly burned out his eyes. He managed to fly home as best he could, but it was a long time before he could see well, and his eyes are red to this day. Then the Hooting Owl and the Horned Owl went, but by the time they got to the hollow tree the fire was burning so fiercely rings burned about their eyes. They had to come home again without the fire, but with all their rubbing they were never able to get rid of the white rings.

Now no more of the birds would venture, and so the little snake, the black racer, said he would go through the water and bring back some fire. He swam across the island and crawled through the grass to the tree, and went in by a small hole at the bottom. The heat and smoke were too much for him, too, and after dodging about blindly over the hot ashes until he was almost on fire himself he managed by good luck to get out again at the same hole, but his body had been scorched black, and he has ever since had the habit of darting and doubling on his track as if trying to escape from close quarters. He came back, and got the great blacksnake, "The Climber" offered to go for fire. He swam over to the island and climbed up the tree on the outside, as the blacksnake always does, but when he put his head down into the hole the smoke choked him so that he fell into the burning stump, and before he could climb out again he was as black as the snake.

Now they held another council, for there was still no fire, and the world was cold, but birds, snakes, and four-footed animals, all had some excuse for not going, because they were all afraid to venture near the burning sycamore, until at last the water spider said she would go. This is not the water spider that looks like a mosquito, but the other one, with black downy hair and red stripes on her body. She can run on top of the water or dive to the bottom, so there would be no trouble to get over to the island, but the question was, how could she bring back the fire? "I'll manage that!" said the Water Spider; so she spun a thread from her body and wove it into a bowl, which she fastened on her back. Then she crossed over to the island and through the grass to where the fire was still burning. She put one little coal of fire into her bowl, and came back with it, and ever since we have had fire, and the Water Spider still keeps her bowl as a design on her back.

Day 3
Wednesday, April 15

Tonight in Albuquerque, the Annual Gathering of Nation's powwow would be starting, bringing in Native Americans from all across the United States and Canada. Television news reports were focused on the large wildland fire burning in the Jemez Mountains. The fire was putting up a smoke column that was visible 10,000 feet up in the atmosphere and could clearly be seen from Albuquerque. This was big news for all the Indians coming in because everyone has a relative involved in the firefighting organization. It is said that being Indian is mainly in your heart. It's a way of walking with the earth instead of upon it. A lot of the history books talk about us Indians in the past tense, but we don't plan on going anywhere... We have lost so much, but the thing that holds us together is that we all belong to and are protectors of the earth; that's the reason for us being here. Mother Earth is not a resource, she is an heirloom.

For Native Americans, powwows are a vital meeting place for the young natives to get noticed by the opposite sex and possibly win some cash if not both. For the much more mature folks it's more of a church, only in the sense that one can go there to get revitalized at being Native. Food is also associated with powwow's, especially Fry-bread.

For those of us on the fire, morale was down because we all knew the pretty women would be looking for new snags tonight, one-night stands. Here we were, stuck up here on this mountain in the heat, sucking up this rugged ash mess. Our thoughts had to be focused on looking out for another kind of snag, one that could kill you if you weren't paying attention. A snag in the fire organization is a dead tree that has ended many a fire-fighters career. Another killer is called a widow-maker. Instead of the whole tree falling, a widow-maker is a dead tree branch falling out of the top of trees. Both can cause serious injury or death to firefighters who don't have situational awareness. When you are in a burned out area with snags, even the slightest breeze should set off an alarm in your head to watch out for falling snags or widow-makers. Sometimes, the fire will burn down into the duff, weakening tree roots without visible signs on the surface of the ground. Any vibration could be enough to cause the snag to fall. Most times you can't even hear it until it's too late.

Day 4
Thursday, April 16

The fourth day drags on until around 5 p.m. when we get a radio call instructing us to secure our immediate area and start patrolling back down toward the staging area. We're told to pick up our supper and prepare to get briefed on our next mission.

When we pulled into the staging area, it didn't look anything like it did when we had first arrived several mornings ago. The place had been transformed into a busy camp. Hotshot buggies sat lined up side by side. A fleet of green engines lined the other side of the road. People were busy setting up small personal camping tents on the outside edge. A dozen huge military tents formed the interior command post.

As we parked and got out, crews started taking notice of our dirty worn out look. You sense a kind of respect as crewmembers start nodding approval, knowing they too would be getting that thousand-yard stare shortly. Most were just glad to get the invite to a big incident and the possibility of scoring another fire T-shirt. On large fire incidents or complexes, in which several fires burn together, this environment will attract t-shirt vendors within a few days. Firefighters are always looking for another cool t-shirt to add to their wardrobe; proof they were at a particular incident and a reminder of people and happenings during the detail.

Dusting ourselves off from the fire, we slowly made our way to the Command Post to check in. A short man was standing behind a desk not much shorter than he was. He put down his handheld radio and looked at a map before peering over his glasses and greeting the incoming crew. He commends us for the valiant effort we put in and tells us to go get some supper and find a place to bed down. We're also told to be ready to hit it hard early tomorrow morning. Briefing will be at 0500 and more details would be available then. He retrieves his radio from the desktop and resumes the conversation he was having when we walked up saying, "What do you mean I

186

can't get those planes here?"

After supper, our crew went back to the engine to sort
out sleeping arrangements. We ended up sleeping
near the engine. The engine boss erected his tent. I
didn't have a tent so I got the seat of the cab. The
other guy put his sleeping bag up on top of the back
section of the engine. It was a major mistake as he
learned around 2 in the morning when he woke up
freezing from contact with the cold steel on the truck
bed making me share the cab with him. Anyway, we
said our good nights and fell immediately into a deep
sleep as the last rays of sunlight slid towards the
horizon.

Day 5
Friday, April 17

The early morning seemed to dawn as soon as our
heads hit the pillow, if you were fortunate enough to
find something to use as such. At any rate, one of the
many duties of the engine boss is to ensure that all of
his crewmembers were up and ready to go to work.

The first business of the day is usually to go visit the
latrine, wash up and go eat breakfast. Morning
briefing followed with roll call. As everyone got their
daily assignments, it seemed that all resources from
the day before were omitted from today's assignment
list. It wasn't until after briefing that the crew got an
explanation of what the Incident Commander (IC)
had in mind for us.

The new IC's strategy was to send the fresh hotshot crews to an old logging road farther north and have them cut a line toward the west flank. He planned to use a fresh strike team (6 engines) of engines to complete the east flank line that our engines had been working on. The fire was also a potential threat to a couple of million-dollar homes located just west of the fire. Our job would be to protect those structures. The command team wanted our engines to join together later with some other engines and possibly create a five to ten person hand-crew.

Crews are called ground resources, each having an equally important role vital to the success of any operation. The progression into fire management usually begins on a hand crew. You then bump up to an engine crew, maybe a Helitack crew or hotshot crew, or on into Smoke-jumping. If you want to move up like most people, you devote your career to one specialty, than become a Fire Management Officer someday just before you retire.

Each engine crew would give up one person as a volunteer for the hand crew. Of course, no one is going to volunteer because everyone knows being on a hand crew is hard work. On my crew, I already knew I would be going. The reasoning was, "Send the new guy, he needs the experience!" Engine folks don't get called engine slugs for no reason; they earn it.

Our hand-crew would be challenged with cutting a

line from the bottom of one road, up the ridge and tying into another log road on top of the mountain. We were trying to protect a power line that was in the path of the fire several mountains over toward the east. The line could also be used as a check line that would slow down the fire progression if the fire started making a westerly run. It wasn't expected to, but this was a good precautionary measure. Protecting those million-dollar homes was top priority. Never mind the trailer park north of the fire, located directly in the path of the fire spread.

I was told this would be good experience, a saying that would ring in my ears throughout my career in fire.

Our newly formed interagency hand-crew gathered at the starting point. Like anything else in fire our ten-person crew ended up being a five person squad. Meanwhile, the engines rolled on up to the top of the mountain to the place we would eventually come out. This is the first time I got re-introduced to an old school mate/best friend of mine. Good ol' Obadi, I hadn't seen him since high school graduation when he left for college on some big athletic scholarship. The last I had heard, he enlisted into the Marines. Now, it appeared he was going to be my crew boss.

As the Division Supervisor introduced the ex-smokejumper, I couldn't help thinking back to those many scouting adventures and the promises we all made growing up. Here he was in the flesh actually "living the dream", a smoke jumper saying. He had truly found a way to support himself by working in the woods. The fire organization just seemed to fit his life style perfectly.

True to his Native nature, he never made eye contact with any of us for fear of one of us stealing his spirit, so he didn't recognize me at first. He was all business and totally in his element. Soon after the introductions, Obadi quickly assigned each individual his spot in the crew. That's when he walks up to me and simply states, "Don't I know you Dawg? " I reply back, "Snake? " Time stopped as we got caught up on 20 years of hiatus in ten minutes. With everyone else attentively watching us, it brought him back to the business at hand. He continued on down the line assessing the experience of each crewmember while glancing back at me and shaking his head.

Seeing how my engine crew had graciously left me with a brand new saw, I was appointed sawyer for this crew. Or, maybe it was because of my Hotshot experience. Anyway, I was the first in line for the time being. Obadi had stated that we would switch off as needed. Next was a strong-looking black guy named Tyron Jackson. Then Obadi placed this cute red head named Sara Jenkins. Bringing up the rear was the clean-up man, Jose Sanchez. Jose was a local resident here in New Mexico and sported a handle bar mustache with a shinny skinned head and tattoos covering his arms. Assignments completed, Obadi turned to re-examine the map. Everyone else started adjusting their packs ensuring they had everything they might need for this assignment.

After the crew boss (Obadi) made radio contact with the IC, he gave the order to move out. We started from the road cutting shrubs and small pinyon trees out of the way and scraping clean a three-foot-wide line down to mineral soil. It was hard work and slow going for five people. About two hours into the operation I was lumbering with the heavy saw. Obadi quickly picked up on this and switched out with a volunteer. It happened to be Ms. Redhead, Sara Jenkins. A girl! As the sun started beating down on us at its highest point in the clear sky, water became valuable and breaks got longer and longer. Even Obadi was showing signs of fatigue as lunch came and went. Our half crew seemed to be ineffective in this thick fuel loading. Except for Sara, who seemed to be in her own element with that saw. Her determination and stamina caused the whole crew, including me, to respect the hell out of this tiny, wiry girl with the heart of a lion, a red lion, a Lioness, pretty red lioness.

As night approached we received a radio transmission instructing us to keep on working into the night and to spike out on the line. Supper was being hiked into us. Tomorrow, a SWIFF (Southwest Indian Firefighter) crew would be linking up with us to complete this assignment. Obadi threw up his hands saying, "It's about time." He turned to walk away as he requested a situation report on the fire.

When he got back, he yelled out, "Break!" Everyone just sat where they were. He came up front, took a seat and got out his pen and writing pad. Looking at the ground for a moment, he put down his pen and pad. Still looking at the ground he said, "Looks like you all are stuck with me for the time being. The fire has over run the Northwest flank and is growing more in this direction. Tomorrow they are shifting resources to this side and changing tactics. We will also be seeing some aircraft on this side. Right now, I just want us to get to know each other better. Sharpen our tools and just get mentally prepared for a long haul. There is no bones about this, it is going to be a not so pleasant assignment. Things are starting to happen too fast, mistakes have been known to occur in this kind of environment. So, John-John, we'll start with you ole son. What got you out here?"

This caught me off guard and it took a moment to gather my thoughts. I stated that "this was my first big fire out west. I had worked on different fire assignments out east. I spent a season with the Asheville Hotshots, a training crew in the mountains of western North Carolina where I had grown up with this guy," (pointing towards Obadi). I shifted around a bit and went on to say I didn't really know what got me here. I guess, like anyone else, I enjoy being outdoors.

To really know me, you would have to know where I came from. My father was half eastern Cherokee and half white. It was hard for me to be accepted into any race. The whites didn't want anything to do with you if you had Indian blood in you. The Indians didn't claim you if you had white in you. So, you're stuck in the middle. Thankfully, my parents were very financially stable. It would have really been tough growing up without friends like Obadi. Yeah, he would kick you down but he wouldn't allow anyone else to pick on you; kind of like we were all his dogs. That's why it was truly fitting to hear he went into the Marines. Plus, I pointed out that I couldn't really go back to the Hotshots after being suspended for fighting a fellow crewmember. I told how it all started on an incident way out in the deep forest. We had hiked nearly five miles to find the dang fire and spent several hours mopping up in a hot, muggy climate. This one guy picked the wrong time to horseplay. He sprayed me down with a bladder bag of water. Soaking wet, I simply got a shovel full of black soot and threw it on him. The fight was on. He rushed towards me, wrapping his arms around my waist. His head was by my stomach so I just started beating on him like a Wildman as we fell backwards.

Obadi says, "Good one, Wildman! Next?" Looking around he finds Tyron and says, "How about you? What got you into fire?"

Tyron laughs, "Me? Shoot man, I have been pushed into all this," waving his arms around the forest. "You guys heard of Boston College, right? Well, back in 1990 I had a full football scholarship until the game with UMASS. I broke my femur, ending my football career. So, I just concentrated on finishing up my degree in biology and got accepted into this apprenticeship program in fire management. This is my first year on an Engine crew. That's about it."

However, he didn't tell how hard it was for him growing up on the streets of Boston's West Side on the other side of the railroad tracks. He didn't tell how his sister had been raped and brutally murdered while coming home from church one sunny Sunday afternoon. No! No one would understand how it felt to be hungry and have nothing to eat for days; to have nothing at all but dreams. Dreams no one could understand but him.

"Pretty good Mr. Boston," Obadi replies. "Now Jose, match that."

"My name is Jose Luis Sanchez, a descendant of the great Aztec warrior, Manuel Luis Sanchez of Mexico. My family has lived here among the pueblo people for centuries. My interest in fire started as a young boy growing up and having to burn off the fields to grow crops. This is my 12th year working for the U.S. Forest Service as a seasonal firefighter. I have worked my way up to Engine captain on the Jemez Ranger District of the Santa Fe National Forest. Thank you!"

He too, cut if off short. True! Jose was born in Mexico. His mom carried him on her back for ten days without water or food, walking across the hot border to reach the United States. He worked his way through school and completed the apprenticeship program in fire management. He was a very hard worker. As engine captain for that district, he kept to himself and was extremely reserved. "Oh, I like to be

194

called Luis, thank you".

"How about Hoser instead," said Obadi. He continued without a pause, "Last but not least, what about you Ms. Red?"

Sara had time to arrange her speech and jumped right in stating, "Ah my name is Sara. You can call me what ever. Red is fine. I uh got interested in fire while in college after having to read "Fire on the Rim." Anyway, that following summer, I filled out an application for the Grand Canyon National Park Helitack crew and got accepted. I have worked there going on two seasons now."

She stopped there for a moment, thinking of sharing how she raced in several triathlons back in California where she was born and raised. Then, she contemplated talking about her close family; about her dad being a pilot for Delta airlines and her mother being a teacher. They both died in an automobile accident caused by a drunk driver one Christmas Eve. She let all that go and off subject said, "I can remember the first day checking in there and seeing a Tall Native American like you with long braids, but mean as hell."

Obadi looks directly at her with a serious look and says, "Are you saying we Indians all look alike to you?" She recoiled back and tried to defend her self by saying, "No, just that you remind me of this person I once met."

Obadi glared back, whispering under his breath, "But you never know! Now listen up you bunch of Hero's. We now know who we all are. All I can say is, if any of you has a problem or sees anything wrong, feels anyway out of the ordinary, don't hesitate to come and talk to me. I want you all to know I have got your back and expect you all to have mine. We came here together and by God we will leave together. Questions? Now, does everyone have headlamps?"

About this time, a couple of our engine crewmembers came stumbling in with two boxes of M.R.E.'s (military meals ready to eat) for each of us. They flopped on the ground and said, "Here're your meals!" Obadi in a matter of fact manner questions them, "What, no hot meals tonight?" We all laughed. They ended up sitting around with us sharing what they heard might be going on. They stated that the rest of our engine crews were sitting on top waiting for us and purposely being our lookouts. But, as they confessed, there seem to be not any good vantage points for this side of the mountain. The road curves back down the other side somewhere, onto private land and was not scouted out. And, they noted that the tree cover gets even denser on up. We asked how far until we reach the road? They tell us it took just over two hours to walk down here. We all slump to the ground after hearing that. Obadi breaks in and says, "Well, that don't surprise me this keeps getting better and better. Sometimes you gotta just say it just doesn't matter."

About this time John asks Obadi, "What about you,

Dawg?"

"Dog gone! Only I can say that. What about me? Let's see I got into fire way back as a kid. Remember me telling you about us kids having to help grandpa burn off his cornfields during the fall? That's when I first got into fire. I went off to college in Kansas, than moved on to Arizona with this girl, who dumped me. I got picked up as a seasonal doing what you are doing John, in the same place. I worked as a Fire tower Lookout one season, moved to the Grand Canyon for a season. I got accepted into the Hotshot program for a couple of seasons, joined the Marines, got discharged and lofted around the southwest doing odd jobs I didn't like. I was accepted into the Jump program, got injured on a bad landing and here I am, back on an engine, still doing this grunt work."

A few minutes pass and Obadi gets up and announces, "The way I see it Dawgs, we are in a hard place, no radio contact, in territory I haven't seen yet, with our engine crew on top as our lookouts and we know help is on the way in the morning. With the firing operations way over several mountains, well we're out of business. Besides, are we not all engine slugs? I suggest you all find a good spot to try and keep warm tonight. It gets pretty nippy out in the elements around 3 a.m."

Day 6
Saturday, April 18

Morning came just as fast as before. We were awakened by the radio blaring throughout the woods informing us that a type II crew, the Jemez crew, was on their way up. That brought all of us to our feet, shaking out the cobwebs of sleepiness. A couple of MRE warming packages were popped open and hot coffee was starting to brew. Smoke lingered in the valley reminding Obadi of the morning mist that rose up off the Great Smoky Mountains back home in North Carolina.

We had just started going back to work around 0630. It was about 0745 when the Jemez crew came snaking up the fire line. It looked pretty impressive to see a fresh crew of 20 red hardhats, dark skinned faces, bright yellow shirts and green pants all in a perfect line carrying saws and hand tools. We all kind of stood aside as the crew boss marched them past us, straight to Obadi.

Obadi quickly recognizes the crew boss and sticks out his hand as he says, "Ah-ho Kevin T. Just when I think this old dog has seen its day, here comes another Kevin T. How you been old Man?"

Kevin recoils from the handshake and turns toward his crew saying, "Oh, I'm still here. I see you're walking better now. Hey, I've got a bunch of green ones this year. It's a new breed. Us old farts are turning over. Heard you needed help, again. Hey, you

198

ever get that Hog or some Jap motorbike?"

Obadi shakes his head no, steps into the fire line to look at the crew and waves. He turns to Kevin and whispers, "You know I don't need any help but they might." Obadi gestured toward us with his lips. The Jemez crewmembers started laughing as if they knew exactly what Obadi was saying to Kevin. Or maybe they were laughing at the gesture he made with his lips, an Indian thing you know. Kevin looked at us on the mountainside and pointed back at Obadi saying, "Jumpers."

After Obadi showed the Jemez crew what to do, they bumped up in front of us and started clearing the way. We fell in behind them and started cleaning up. It worked out so much easier and faster that way.

Just before lunchtime we tied into the road. What a relief! It was a blessing to see our engines and the rest of the crew sitting on top of the individual Engines drinking cold cokes.

As Obadi, Kevin and all the rest of the engine bosses met around the hood of one engine. The rest of us reintegrated back into our own crew; the Jemez-crew just stood lined up, on the road, with some of them leaning on their tools. Others were drinking pop the engine guys had tossed to them. All of us were facing outward looking off the road toward the smoke column.

When the group checked in with the IC by radio, he

relayed that the type II crew could continue on up the road and tie in with Division G (golf). The fire had been divided up into divisions now. This makes it easier to manage, meaning the fire continues to grow larger. The IC also wanted the strike team of engines to head back to base camp and start preparing needed equipment for an extensive progressive hose lay. That means unrolling and laying 2 1/2-inch diameter synthetic water hose for as far as 10 miles in the most severe scenarios.

We planned to start first thing tomorrow morning, relaying that if we could catch and contain the west flank today with the hotshots doing their burnout, we would throw everything left tomorrow on the east flank. If the tanker planes would hammer the flaming front in the north with slurry, it should slow it down so we could get the flanks contained. We needed the west secured because of multi-million-dollar homes on that side. Again, we weren't concerned with the trailer park just to the north with the main fire heading straight for it. Even in fire, there are politics. Politics dictate that resources to protect should be prioritized by the most costly property that is owned by the highest paying taxpayers. Of course politicians don't take into consideration the tax break imposed on these high value homeowners and the fact that they have insurance coverage for any loss.

Anyway, that was our assignment. As you learn in this culture, in the heat of battle you don't question the task. You get it done. That's the can do attitude that has changed over the years. You learn from experience it can get you and or someone else seriously injured, if not killed.

We all loaded up in our respected engines and started lumbering slowly back down the old logging road. It made me wonder what it must have been like traveling this terrain in an old wagon train. We had nice comfortable seats, shock absorbers, rubber tires and a lot of horsepower. It felt cool under the green canopy of trees and a nice breeze was blowing up the ridge from the flat valley below. We sat in total silence listening to the radio and continuing to pick up conversations about the fire activity on the other side. All of the sudden, the driver slammed on the brakes just in time to allow a family of four deer and two small bears to cross the road in front of us. It was as if they were all traveling together and not frightened of us at all. A small doe stopped momentarily to glance in our direction before scampering off to catch up with the rest. It reminded me of the Native stories Obadi had shared with me when we were kids. At that moment I wished I could have lived during that time of peace with all living things.

Arriving at the base camp, we got back into the fire mode. We took a quick inventory of what we already had on the engine and what items we might need. When that was done we proceeded toward the incident command post to check in and get briefed on our next assignment. Two of the other engine crews were still messing around with gear laid out all around their engines. They were arguing over small details. Obadi's crew sat in one corner lounged out with hands folded behind their heads and legs stretched out and crossed. They were watching everyone walk in and out of the tent as if they owned the place. Obadi spoke up, "What took you all so long, Dog?" I say, "Inventory!" He fires back, "They still don't have an inventory list taped to the inside of those compartments? Gee, I mentioned that way back when. Now we have to wait on those other rookies to dick around."

The Incident Commander turned around from the wall map and told us, "Yeah why don't you all go ahead leave those inventories here and go get cleaned up, get something to eat, rest up and we will start fresh tomorrow morning. We'll know more of the details at the morning briefing. Thanks of the valiant effort." That's all we needed to hear. We all raced straight toward the showers. The camp was mostly dead like a western ghost town. We did see the staff that works to prepare the camp. We call them the camp crew. If you ever get to experience the environment of a huge fire camp you will learn to appreciate the smaller comforts we take for granted at home. I mean luxuries like a nice long hot private shower, no waiting in lines or having to hurry up so everyone can get a little hot water and a nice clean flush toilet. But, with experience, you learn ways to make the best of it in any given situation. If you don't know, observe the old timers, the seasoned firefighters. They won't share secrets of the trade. They save it all for their own comfort.

After showering, we set up our tents that had been checked out from supply to finally get some much-needed rest. If you're ever privileged enough to get time off and try to sleep during the day in a big base camp you'll learn quickly it is nearly impossible with all the noise and aircraft working nearby. Well impossible, unless you are too tired to notice, as we were.

Day 7
Sunday, April 19

Morning came with the engine boss shaking the tents and whispering to see if we were awake. Of course, you show some movement just to acknowledge his presence. But, like the elementary school days, you lay still wishing this was all a bad dream and you could just ignore him, roll over and go back to sleep. But, as hard as you try, you can't tune out all the noises from everyone else camped around you. You soon realize you have no choice but to get moving. It isn't hard waking up after that initial call because everyone knows the duties expected. It's all about fire once again. The nice dreams you might have had fade away as reality sets in and you realize the hellhole you're truly in. This is where you realize that not everyone is capable of doing this kind of work, not when you could have a nice cozy bed and a warm woman to snuggle up with. In this business it's just you and the elements to deal with.

In fire camp you do everything as a crew. You arrive

as a crew. You camp as a crew. You shower as a crew. You eat as a crew and you leave as a crew. That's why it's a little better arriving as an engine crew. You only have to deal with the three you arrived with, not the twenty if you are on a hand crew.

Breakfast is always a wait in line, but well worth it. In the world of wildland firefighting you quickly learn the ropes. One of your first observations will be how well you're fed in fire camp. They feed you as if it was going to be your last meal. For some people, this occupation is very attractive and probably the best they could hope for. We eat in Army tents with folding tables and chairs. Coffee is the most memorable thing about any base camp, thick as mud and black as night but just the right kick to get you going again.

After grabbing a food tray, you stop by the beverage counter and then find a seat. Usually crewmembers sit together unless you see someone you recognize from another fire detail. In that case, if you go sit by your old acquaintance and your crew will usually congregate around you. Then, you can make introductions and share the story of how you first met this old acquaintance. That's how the circle of friendship continues in fire. Next year you will do the same and the circle will continue throughout your career until soon you notice you are the elite everyone is talking about. It all starts in these fire-camps. Another observation that's hard to miss is when crews show off their colors. Every crew wears their color t-shirts to the mess tent. Some of the interagency crews don't have colored t-shirts so they wear their yellow nomex shirts. All these different groups of colored t-shirts will be sitting together. Their appearance sometimes resembles a gang.

Morning briefing is usually held before or during breakfast. A lot of times it's still dark and, as stated before, not everyone is expected to attend. Attendance is mandatory for the division supervisors and bosses. Important logistical information is shared at these briefings and it's expected to be passed along to crews and other subordinates prior to getting out on the fire line. The information will include expected weather conditions, assignments, local hazards, and the fire situation report, just to name a few. Firefighters also place a heavy emphasis on knowing L.C.E.S. (Lookouts, Communication, Escape Routes, and Safety Zones). That was the topic of conversation when I saw Obadi standing stoic as ever, arms folded, looking up at the incident commander and listening attentively to every word. I walked up, nudged him in the side saying, "o-se-o," the Western Cherokee saying for hello. He quickly corrected me with a, "she-yo," the Eastern Cherokee saying for hello. I should have known that and quickly recognized it. "Say, what's the word?" I inquire. Obadi turns towards me answering, "Haven't you all heard? I think they want our strike team to stick together and do structure protection on those million dollar homes. But we'll see, let's listen to the rest of the briefing. As the briefing wound down, it was apparent our strike team would be together.

We spent the rest of the early morning hours loading up 1,200 feet of soft line hose and the needed fittings for our structure protection task. By 0700 all the engines in the strike team were rolling out of base camp heading toward the million dollar homes.

We arrived in the suburbs of the residential area to find residents already gathering up personal belongings and being evacuated out of their own neighborhoods.

Our task was to assess what homes we thought we could defend with the water capacity in our engine. If a house was deemed "non-defendable," a red rock was placed in the driveway, marking it as such. Several factors were considered when making decisions on which houses we would attempt to save. Construction materials, defensible space around the house, and value were major determining factors.

A dozer line had already been constructed in front of the homes in our assigned subdivision. We removed or spread out flammable fuels located around the houses so embers from the flaming front would not ignite the property. Garden hoses were stretched out and placed on rooftops. Water was turned on so the hoses would soak down the roofing material. Brush was cut away from the homes.

We took our first break around lunchtime and sat down in the shade of the engine trying to escape the blistering sun. Everyone ate in silence, listening to the radio traffic and soaking up every tidbit of information on what was going on closer to the fire. After about an hour we were startled awake by the radio once again. The division supervisor called our engine number checking on our progress with the assignment. Time had slipped by us, and we realized our little lunch break had turned into a nice siesta.

A light haze of smoke replaced the calm blue sky as we all started getting up and moving around. The division supervisor was saying things had taken a turn for the worse. He was sending two hotshot crews our way. The rest of the strike team was to try and defend these houses. The flame front was moving in our direction. We were told to get on a section of the dozer line and chase any spot fires between the houses and the dozer line. We would be trying to "hold the line."

With that, the engine boss signed off. We all grabbed hand tools and rushed to the dozer line. By now, we could see heavy smoke boiling over the ridge top. A low flying DC 3 came roaring over head making the hair stand up on the back of my neck. About this same time, a hotshot crew marched up the dozer line past us and continued on over the ridge. We felt helpless; just the three of us standing around waiting for this natural enemy to come our way unleashing its fury. A few moments later another hotshot crew marched past us in silence and continued out of sight. Finally, off in the distance behind us in the direction our engine was parked, we could see other engine lights positioning around the different houses. We felt a little better but still didn't know what to expect. The smoke got thicker and thicker until visibility was limited to only a few feet away. A long time passed with no radio transmissions. We continued to stand and sit around on our tools waiting for any kind of word. We were spaced out about a hundred feet from each other. Another engine crew soon joined us.

Out of the thick smoke, the hotshot crews re-appeared like apparitions marching back past us in total silence with a look of defeat on their faces. Suddenly, the dark cloud of smoke turned orange and embers started falling all around us. Everyone raced around feverishly trying to extinguish the numerous spot fires popping up everywhere as a result of the flying embers. Looking back, we could see the flames torching out over the tree line on top of the ridge.

Someone on our ridge yelled for us to get up to the house. "Work the house!" We started running up hill and kept falling down in the thick brush. The house we were assigned to protect was only a few hundred feet up hill from the dozer line we were on. Now, it seemed to take forever to get to it. As we got closer we could see another house nearby starting to ignite.

Since I was the first to arrive at the top, I raced toward the engine and started going through the motions of turning on the pump. There are steps to follow and valves to be turned off and priming/pumping water into the system before it can work properly. By the time I was done with that, one of the other guys came staggering up beside the engine. Breathless, he leaned over asking, "Is it ready?" I ran past him and said, "Watch the pump," as I raced to find the nozzle. The engine boss was standing by the house talking on the radio. He too was winded and leaning over. He pointed for me to direct the water on the brush just in front of the house. I had just reached the brush when he hollered to "pull out." I whirled around and saw him giving a hand signal to cut and run. I dropped the hose, ran back and jumped in the engine as it was pulling away.

Back at the main road we regrouped with everyone else in a large field. We had clear sky over our heads once again. Everyone was getting out and high five-ing each other on a close call. I didn't get it. We sat the rest of the afternoon watching the air show as tanker planes hammered the mountain with slurry drops, painting the landscape a bright orange. A smoke column boiled upward for thousands of feet. We could tell our lines were not holding this beast in check at all. We felt helpless.

It was around 1800 or 6 p.m. before we got word to head back to base camp to get supper, shower and crawl into our tents. For a few hours our minds would be free to dream of things in the outside world.

Day 8
Monday, April 20

This morning we reviewed the IAP (Incident Action

Plan) and learned our strike team was assigned to the same area. The IAP is updated each day before the first shift begins and contains important information about weather, fire activity, available resources, assignments, known hazards, safety etc. Today, since the fire had already moved on, we would be tasked with cleaning up the aftermath of destruction. That includes cutting down any hazardous trees and mopping up (putting out) hot spots. Rumor had it that the news media would be touring the area sometime in the afternoon.

The first glimpse of the subdivision confirmed our fears from the day before; not much was saved. The landscape was scorched black and resembled a moonscape. We pulled up to the location of our assigned house. Surprisingly, it was one of few spared from destruction. To our amazement, the fire had burned around the property and torched adjacent houses.

Obadi's crew was a little farther down the road from us. He requested our help in cutting some trees around their area. We met up with him and he showed us what to do. According to safety regulations, we had to be paired up. I was the odd man on our crew so he teamed up with me.

We started by the old wooden barn that was half burned. There was a snag leaning toward the structure that needed to be felled. He asked if I felt comfortable cutting it. Being an ex-hot shot, I told him it would be no problem.

I assessed the dead tree and planned to do my cuts in a manner that should cause the snag to fall away from the barn. A sawyer can usually put a tree on the ground where he wants it if the cuts are done right. Everything was going fine until the wind picked up. Just as the snag started to fall, it twisted and smashed right on top of the remaining structure collapsing it to the ground. My mouth just dropped as Obadi pushed me to the down hill side of the mountain, just out of sight of the white news van passing by. All the other engine folks started laughing and took cover themselves. Walking back toward the others, Obadi patted me on the back and said to the others, "He damn sure is a wildman." Thus was born the nickname, Wildman.

Day 9
Tuesday, April 21

Morning briefing revealed that today our strike team would be working with one the local helicopters. We would continue mopping up in the multi-million-dollar subdivision. It now bore little resemblance to the lavish luxury living it once was. Since Obadi and Sara were the aviation experts on our team, they were delegated as the two contacts.

Working around helicopters requires good communication. One crucial thing to remember when working under the aircraft is to talk to the pilot in terms of his perspective; "I am at your 12 o'clock," not, "You are at <u>my</u> 12 o'clock." It's just easier and quicker for you on the ground to see the helicopter than it is for the pilot to look for you. You will definitely hear the aircraft before you see it. Kind of like you will smell the smoke before you see it.

Air attack requires additional safety concerns for firefighters on the ground. Crew bosses have to ensure all personnel are clear and on the uphill side, before a bucket drop occurs. This tactic diminishes the danger of the water drop breaking something loose that might fall on firefighters and injure them. Air attack is really helpful when doing initial attack or mop up in inaccessible places.

At 0830 the pilot radioed saying he was two minutes out. Everyone hurried to back away from a hot spot we had been working for the last hour-and-a-half. Soon we could hear the thumping of his rotor blades. As he crested the ridge we were on, he called for Sara by name, "Babe where do you want it?" She expertly answered back, "Sierra PaPa-23 I am at your two o'clock". The pilot slowed the copter to a hover and confirmed, "Got you." Sara replied, "Good. We need the drop on the heavy smoke in the direction I am pointing, confirm?" The pilot quickly answers back. As the copter begins to move in the direction that Sara is pointing, the pilot says, "Easy enough, signal for the release." About that same time Sara radio's back, "Release!" A full load of about 350 gallons of pond water comes ripping through the burned out trees tearing down everything in its path.

Only moments before, the helicopter had appeared with its load. Now, you could just barely catch a glimpse of the pilot looking down as the ship pulled up and away. When the noise faded out of earshot, everyone rushed back in to work the sizzling ground.

As we started to turn the earth over we noticed something strange. It was Sara who let out the first scream. As she bent down to examine what was moving in the muck, a bunch of dying fish started to flop around among the crew. Everyone jumped and ran away screaming bloody murder. The damn pilots had scooped up a school of fish from the nearby pond. Obadi walked over to Sara and extended his hand saying, "Great catch, Red!" Sara looked up. "That's it. I do remember you. You're the one who gave me such a hard time checking in at the Crescent Ranger District, way back when. I think you were just recovering from that jump accident. I remember uh something I said about not wanting to be with the broke down engine that year and you thought I meant "Injun." You got all irate." Obadi rebounded for the moment by whispering, "Na!" Sara continued, "Oh yes you did." Looking around at the rest of us she added, "He about made me piss on myself yelling at me. You do not want to piss this guy off, I can tell you." Obadi butted in, "But we became best of friends." Sara huffed, "Yeah, after you confessed you were just joking!"

That night at base camp rumors started floating around about the infamous frogman being scooped out of a lake and dumped on a fire somewhere in

California by a helicopter bucket drop. Supposedly, a man was scuba diving when a fire broke out several miles away. The local suppression crew needed to use the closest water source, which happened to be the very lake the man had chosen to scuba dive. As the helicopter crew dropped the bucket to fill with water, they accidentally scooped up the scuba diver and dropped him into the fire. Several days later a crew was mopping up and ran across this dead scuba diver out in the middle of the forest, many miles from the nearest lake. Only one conclusion could be drawn from this.

This is one of many stories you are likely to hear in a fire camp. Is it true? Well, it depends on who you talk to, another example of the culture.

Day 10
Wednesday, April 22

This morning I decided to go check out the morning briefing. It's open to all but mainly the crew bosses attend. It starts at 0500 when most of the crewmembers are just starting to wake up. It's still dark! But, it's a pretty neat experience.

As you walk up to the big tent where the briefing is held, you can barely make out dark figures mingling around in tight groups drinking steaming cups of coffee. Laughter and teasing can be heard all around. Light from inside streams out through the flaps. You can make out rows of chairs with people sitting in them. A podium stands alone in the center perched atop a makeshift stage at the front. Maps line the back wall depicting the fire perimeter and how it has grown. Safety messages hang all around the other end reminding firefighters of important rules to follow. They're known as "Fire Orders" and "Watch-out Situations."

I grab a cup of coffee and walk around until I run into Obadi talking to this mean looking Mexican guy named Sanchez. He was one of the guys in our strike team of engines. He didn't seem to have much to say to anyone but he and Obadi appeared to hit it off okay. I would find out later that he was one of Obadi's marine buddies. He loved talking about a 1934 Ford pickup his father had left him and how he was fixing it up. It was another tight brotherhood like the bond I had experienced with Ashville IHC (Interagency Hotshot Crew). It's something you can't explain to anyone else unless they have experienced it. It's an unspoken respect.

I walked up behind the two acting like I accidentally bumped into Obadi who leaned forward a little, protecting his coffee with one hand to keep it from spilling all over the place. If looks could kill, that look he momentarily shot my way said it all. I couldn't help but bust up laughing saying, "Ohhh I'm sorry!" Sanchez was the one to speak first blurting out, "Pingchee Ka-Roan" in Spanish. Obadi regained his composure, "That's all right! That's all right. I know ya. I know where you live Dog; your sisters; your mom; all of them!" On that note we all laughed and started surveying the tent.

One thing I realized about Obadi; he was one of those people that didn't like to stand out in a crowd but always managed to do so by his actions. He would always be in the back row standing with a crowd of friends by him. The one's attracted to him were always the misfits and underdogs of society, or so they seemed. You see them around, like biker dudes; mean to the bone. To know Obadi, he wasn't like that. Paul Gleason, the hotshot leader, once said that leaders had to be born because a good leader had to have an innate ability to be mindful of others. He said it's something you can't develop. Either you have it or you don't. It gave me something to ponder.

As we begin conversing, Obadi reintroduced Sanchez to me as another "hotheaded hotshot." Sanchez retorted, "Aren't we all?" Obadi jumped in asking, "How are you liking, engine work?" I responded back that I wasn't getting to do much. Sanchez remarks, "What?" Obadi was just about to say something else when he got interrupted by the loudspeaker and the IC standing at the podium saying, "Okay, okay, let's get this show on the road." Obadi leaned over and whispered, "Talk to me after this." I shook my head in acknowledgement.

The morning briefing lasted a good hour. It covered everything; crew roll call, weather, fire behavior, aviation support, communication, medical concerns, safety issues and the IC summary in which he thanked everyone for his or her supportive efforts.

With that out of the way, everyone adjourned outside to find their division supervisor and get further instructions for individual tasks to be completed on the fire-line.

This is when Obadi catches up with me and asks if I want some real experience working on an engine. I ask, "What do you mean?" He tells me Sanchez has a Type 3 Engine and says one of his guys is sick. Obadi suggests that maybe I could be switched over for the day." I answer, "Sure!" Before I got back to my own engine crew they already knew about it. The switch didn't present a problem since we were all working together anyway. I would just be getting some experience on a bigger Type 3 Engine with five crewmembers.

Sanchez ran a tight ship. One look at the engine and you could see it was kept up with pride. Everything had its own place. After several days on this fire, this engine still looked neat. The crewmembers even carried an air of confidence. I was put in the middle back seat, the number 5 spot.

Each seat position had a special designated duty on the engine. When the engine rolled up to an incident my first job was to jump out and open compartment number three which was located on the left side. I would grab a progressive hose pack with three 1-1/2 inch forestry nozzles and run to the end of the hose that had been quickly laid out in a specific direction by the number-three man. The number-two man, the driver, would chock the wheels and operate the pump.

Sanchez was the number-one man. He would direct the necessary changes and be our radio contact person/Engine Boss. The number-four man was the helper and hose connector. Unfortunately, our division was in mop up mode and we probably wouldn't get the chance to go through this drill.

Again, we were sent back into the subdivision to continue mopping up. A firefighter can only take so much of boring, tedious, dirty, mop-up detail. After all, we're firefighters; we want to be where the action and excitement is!

Sanchez and I just weren't hitting it off. I felt like he was looking down at me and had me pegged as a "rich white boy." And, I guess my arrogant attitude didn't help matters much. Every time he cut me down, I always had something to fire back at him. Our antics made the crewmembers crack up but I could tell Sanchez wasn't amused. But, that was my personality. I learned to be that way from my younger years trying to hang out with Obadi's gang of troublemakers.

Around 2 p.m. we went to refill the engine using a neighborhood fire hydrant. The job wouldn't require everyone's effort so I grabbed the hydrant wrench and got ready to open it up. Sanchez just happened to be on top checking the porthole.

One of the crewmembers tossed him one end of the fill hose and threw the other end my way. I wrestled around with it for a while before finally getting it

218

connected. Looking it over, I said, "I guess that's right." Sanchez became impatient, stood up and blurted, "Will someone for God's sake help this fool?" In rebuttal I confirmed, "I got it! I got it!" Sanchez bent back down and looked into the tank saying, "Well let her rip!"

Not knowing the pressure, I turned the valve wide open as fast as I could. The force of the water sent Jose Luis Sanchez into the air desperately trying to hang on to the wild hose that was shooting water everywhere. To my amazement he did stay on top but got drenched from head to toe. He was so mad he couldn't even speak. He just glared at me as he climbed off the engine and duck-stepped past me. I wanted to run but I had no place to go. All I could say was, "Sorry."

That night at supper Obadi came over to sit with all of us. The first thing he did was to look over at Sanchez and say, "Hoser ah, I mean Jose what happened man?" Everyone busted up laughing and by morning the whole camp knew Jose as Hoser.

Day 11
Thursday, April 23

After supper last night, around 8:00 or so, Obadi broke out some cards and announced, "Who's up for a game of cards?" I guess he sensed the so-called ten-day lag. It's a period during camp when no one wants to be there anymore. As Sun Tzu states in the book "Art of War", this is the most vulnerable period of combat. "When your forces are dulled, your edge is blunted, your strength is exhausted, and then others will take advantage of this."

Anyway, a bunch of us went over to the dining tents where there was light and tables for our use. The interest was overwhelming. We set one table up front in the middle and left the two rows of tables running down the sides. New players took up a table behind the last and latest game on either side. The winner advanced up to the next table until you reached the front center table game to face off for the grand table. The loser had to either start over at the back or simply walk out. It was about 1 a.m. when the IC came in and ended it, sending everyone to bed.

At the morning briefing the weatherman announced that an inversion was expected to hang over the region today. That didn't mean too much for those of us who were inexperienced at that time, but it will from here on out. Everyone in charge agreed that today was a window of opportunity to take advantage of and get into those hot and hard-to-get-to isolated spots. Obadi and several others protested to deaf ears about playing with people's lives here. Those in charge were focused on getting the job done. Perhaps that's why our strike team was assigned to one of the main problem areas.

The division supervisor needed for us to Re-form that five-man hand-crew we had last week. The Jemez crew needed a few bodies to fill in because several of their own folks were incapacitated with the camp crud, otherwise known as a stomach sickness usually caused by poor hygiene. Large camps are prime areas for the crud. There are lots of people living in a small area sharing the same facilities and germs/viruses can be easily spread. Once a sickness gets started, it can soon affect the whole camp.

We were put on the tail end of the Jemez crew. If things went like the last time we worked together, this was going to be a piece of cake. Besides, all we were doing was widening a fire-line that was already in place. It was the same one we had worked on during that first week to protect a power line running side slope. A hotshot crew would be working from the bottom up and we were to ride our engine up to the top and work down toward the hotshot crew; building fire-line downhill, a watch-out situation. Man, were we up for this assignment. We weren't going to let this hotshot crew show us up, "A Type two crew? No way!" So we started out fast and hard making headway and progressing a good distance down. We found out later that the hotshot crew was thinking we were just a regular Type II crew and didn't expect us to get as far as we did. With that in mind, they waited until mid morning to begin working uphill toward us. The morning inversion caused the smoke to stay heavy in the valley, making visibility less than a few feet away. It also made working in it even harder because of all the carbon monoxide being breathed in. To mitigate this we had to start taking more and more breaks.

During one of our long extended breaks, Tyron came over to Obadi and I singing an unfamiliar tune. He plopped down, crossed his leg in front of Obadi and straight out asked, "Hey dude, tell me about jumping out of perfectly good airplanes?" Obadi was leaning back on his day-pack, legs extended out and crossed, taking in the needed break as well. He leaned up, crossed his leg like Tyron and replied," Just about jumping or about how I got screwed up?" Tyron smiled and said, "Shoot man, that's what I was leading up to. I hear all these cats talking behind your back. I just want to hear it from you, the real thing. Man, you know what I mean?" Obadi paused for a moment and said, "Yeah, I can respect that," looking directly back at Tyron under his squinting eyes. Tyron answered, "Yeah man, then I could tell these mothers to shut the hell up for you." Obadi replied "All right then!"

He told how it took him three seasons of applying just to get accepted into a candidate spot for Smoke Jumping. They train candidate's hard everyday trying to weed out the ones that have attitude problems. It's no joke. It's kind of like boot camp; so regimental that by the time you get your first jump you're so busy going through each proper sequence that by the time you think about it, your parachute is opening and you are on your way to the ground. And what a scary feeling it is to fall! I think everyone is scared the first few times out; you know the fear of the unknown. Reasoning you will either be alive and happy or it just wouldn't matter anyway in less than a minute. That's why you can't exactly remember what you were thinking at that very moment.

He continued, "We had gotten a call to jump a fire up in Washington State somewhere near the town of Twisp Washington. It had been the start of a busy fire season and we had jumped one 70-acre fire that morning only to turn it over to the district folks and head back to the airbase. We had just enough time to swap out our used chutes and grab another out of the bin when the alarm went off again. It was our signal to get ready and load up the plane again. In training, you have to get used to suiting up within two minutes. So, when the alarm sounds, everyone drops what they are doing and makes haste toward the ready room."

"We get suited and load up. Within fifteen minutes, the plane is taxiing down the runway of Winthrop, Washington a small booster jump base. About 20 minutes into the flight we can see the smoke column leaning over a bit. The pilot gets our attention and points it out. He holds up two fingers meaning 20 mile an hour wind speed. Not good! The pilot holds up both arms not sure what we want to do, because by the book we are not supposed to jump with wind speeds over 15 miles an hour. The spotter has the authority to make this decision. Jumper's are known for having this can do attitude so we all knew the answer before the spotter could signal back the answer hell yes we will jump. As we circle the fire a few times everyone is looking out the side windows sizing it up. The spotter leans out the door looking for a good spot for us to jump. I kind of had this funny feeling not exactly wanting to jump. Call it gut instincts. I was seated fifth from the door, which meant if the usual number of four jumpers were called to jump this small fire I would be all right. I would be first up the next call out. The spotter soon throws two streamers out the door to test the winds. He talks to the pilot making the plane do a little adjustment and we start to circle around again. We're all glued to the windows desperately trying to see where the streamers are landing. The first streamer misses the mark. Looking down, we could see a lot of dead snags and rock ledges where the first set of streamers landed. I think to myself, just my luck. The second pair of streamers landed near a small opening on the top of the same ridge where the fire was cresting. That was about as good as it was going to get. If you missed the spot and continued on over the ridge, you would drop way down into this canyon. If you landed short, there was another steep canyon with a rock face, not much room for error."

The spotter leans back in and as we are trained to do, we look at him with our hands over our reserve chutes waiting to see how many jumpers will be needed. He holds up two fingers. I sit back in relief. Two jumpers stand up, hook up and head toward the door, one right behind the other in position to leap out. The spotter checks the area one last time and leans back in with a hard slap on the leg of the first jumper. A loud snapping sound of ruckus and just like that, the two jumpers disappeared out the door. The plane banked into another circle and we could see the chutes having a hard time in the wind.

The first two jumpers missed the jump spot and one landed in a patch of snags. The spotter curses under his breath and holds up two more fingers. The jumper in front of me turns to face me and, says 'He's determined to kill someone today.' Then, he gets up, goes through the routine hooked up, gets in a ready stance, gets the slap on the leg and exits. This time the spotter hangs out the door longer then pounds on the floor of the plane. The plane begins another turn. We can see one of the chutes malfunctioning. The spotter waves for the next two to quickly get ready. Not being able to see what was going on, we knew this was urgent. As I get into position the spotter looks me in the face and shouts, 'You come up short, you die; you go long, you die! You understand?' I am shaking my head as he says, 'Good, get ready' and slap, I'm out in the wild blue yonder thinking, what the hell? I try focusing on my counts when I quickly notice my feet are straight up and my parachute is opening. A big hard yank and a popping sound made me realize something wasn't right. I had no sooner noticed all that, when a violent jerk snapped me upright. But my helmet and head were being forced down. I could see my daypack tumbling toward earth."

"We have procedures and counts for everything, even on our way down. You have to be thinking to survive. In one of my leadership classes I learned there are no perfect survival stories. Some fumble around and get it right making it out alive. This is what I was going through."

"The first part of my sequence was already screwed up and there was no going back. However, I knew I had about 22 seconds after I exited the plane to take action or use my reserve chute. Time was ticking. We are trained and go through all the possible malfunctions we may encounter on our way down learning how to quickly mitigate them. It was common for me in recent days to deploy my chute with a few twists. All you have to do is pull your riser out to your side and scissor-kick out of the twist until you can look up and see a full canopy. Thinking this was just a bad one, I pulled and kicked and kicked and kicked too damned long."

"When I finally got a full canopy I was breaking treetops as I came crashing down through the timber. Crossing my arms so they wouldn't get broke I closed my eyes just as a violent jerk brought the realization that I had survived. Swearing out loud to be alive I next started to go through the motions of doing a let-down. That's the procedures we jumpers are taught to get down from a tall pine tree. On the right side of our Jump pants leg pocket we carry a 120-foot rope. That is looped around a D ring on our jump suits and we tie off to the tightest riser of our now entangled parachute lines. Then we simply detach ourselves from the parachute and repel toward the ground. But once I went through all the procedures and was ready to repel down nothing happen. As I look around retracing the procedures I saw that part of the suit was caught on a branch of the tree. As I freed the suit the weight dropped me down a bit as the line took up the slack causing the one limb the parachute was caught on to give way.

This sent me free-falling all the way to the ground crashing through the branches that my jump bro could hear way on up the mountain. The next thing I realized, I was looking up at the clear blue sky again. Every now and then a puffy white cloud would pass by. All was quiet and I couldn't or dared not move. It felt as if all the wind was knocked out of me and I couldn't get enough air back into my lungs but I couldn't move a thing. I remember thinking, "What the hell just happened?" This all seemed as if I had been here before. I finally faded off to sleep or passed out. I saw images of "Frisky," my favorite dog I had grown up with. My grandpa with grandma seem to be shaking their heads back and forward as if to be saying poor thing. I remember it being so quiet and peaceful. I came to when my other jumper bros tried to move me, or at least bend my legs straight out from under me. I reckon I had no feeling because all the tendons and nerve endings were torn from the bone. They say I was the lucky one. Two other bros didn't fare so well. The initial attack call, turned into a rescue mission on that day. It took several hours into the night before my bros could haul me up to the nearest logging road where a forest service rig carried me on down to a waiting ambulance on the Highway. I'll never forget the painful ride down that old logging road feeling every painful bump. I also had a very hard time sleeping and rehabilitating after that accident. It took almost a year, several painful operations and a lot of hard rehab work to get me on my feet again. But here I am back out here."

A gentle breeze blows up from the valley. Tyron shakes his head and asks, "Why? It seems like you are a hard one to learn!" Obadi sits for a moment then begins to get up saying, "Why? I love it! Besides, three strikes you are out, some-day you'll see me riding away on my Hog." Sanchez throws in, "Or a custom 34 Ford pickup." Obadi laughs and states "Either, or!"

We went back to work digging line, feeling a little funny. Obadi stayed on the ground a little longer. We continued past lunchtime trying to make it to the spot we camped at the first week. That would be well past the half way mark. Around 2 p.m., Kevin the Jemez crew boss, hollered back, "Lunch!" Everyone remained where they were. Obadi walked down and met Kevin in the middle of all of us. They sat down uphill from the line. The smoke was starting to lift up out of the valley.

The smoke here on the slopes wasn't any better. We couldn't see the guys on either end. Everyone started fumbling around in their daypack checking to see what kind of sack lunches had been sent with us from camp. We all looked like bandits removing our bandanas from around our face. That's all we had to protect our airways from the smoke. We had to leave our goggles on because if we didn't, our eyes would quickly tear up. Everyone tried to make the best of it but you could still hear protests about the working conditions.

Obadi and Kevin broke out the cards again and resumed the match that was interrupted the night before. Little by little, a small group started to congregate around the game.

Most however, stayed put and talked in their language. They would laugh from time to time and talk a little more in their language. I used this time to get to know Red a little better. I had my eye on her from the first day we were introduced. She was a pretty neat person; someone you could tell was determined to go places. She was strong-willed, but petite and lady like; quiet, reserved, but opinionated. She carried an air of confidence that gained her respect. Anyway, I could tell she had no interest in getting involved with someone like me. We just talked about our goals and dreams.

An hour and a half went by and the card-game was still in full swing. Loud laughter of Ooohs and Ahhhs as the hands were dealt. Finally out of the noise, Kevin announces, "That's it! Back to work!" Some of the guys remark "Sore loser!" as they put their gear back on.

We barely got started when someone yelled, "Broken tool, boss!" Kevin walked back uphill to the disgruntled crewmember and handed him his own tool saying, "Don't think you're getting out this that quick." Everyone burst out laughing.

A breeze is starting to pick up, blowing up from the

valley. The smoke is drifting up slope. Obadi makes his way down around the crew and talks to Kevin at the front. He informs Kevin that maybe someone should go down and see exactly where the hotshot crew is and how much farther we have to go. Kevin agrees, sending Obadi on down the fire-line.

Obadi walks for almost an hour before he reaches the old campsite. He continues another hour before he reaches the hotshot crew sitting around on the fire-line. This makes Obadi mad as he quickens his pace straight toward the superintendent in charge.

As he closes the gap, the hotshot superintendent sees him and yells for everyone to get back to work. Obadi yells out toward no one in particular," Who's running this charade?" He recognizes the young superintendent and motions for him to follow as they continue on down the fire-line. Obadi starts, "How long have we known each other?" The young superintendent replies, "For awhile now, of course what's up?" Obadi continues, "Well here's what's up. You got my guys busting butt, working downhill to meet your hotshots. I get here and find you all messing around, not even half way. Don't bullshit me. I know how far a good shot crew can work on this type of assignment. You better get your boys on the move. A type II crew is about to show your guys up. I wouldn't want that on my head. Got it?" The superintendent was about to say something back but Obadi had already turned and headed back up the mountain. Just before he disappeared into the tree line Obadi stops again. Yelling back he asks, "By the way

230

where is your lookout?" The superintendent yells back, "I thought you were going to use the engines as your lookouts?" Obadi throw up both arms as he replies back, "I am!! On my end watching that end! Who the hell is watching this end?" A long silence falls over the area as everyone stops moving and starts looking at the superintendent. Finally the superintendent moves to pick up his gear, shouting "I'm on it! Don't worry!" Obadi disappears into the forest yelling out "Rookie!"

On his way back up, the smoke started to lift and visibility got a little better, enough for him to tell the fire was closer to the line than anticipated. At that moment things started deteriorating quickly. All of the sudden the wind picked up, blowing embers across the fire-line. Obadi says to himself out loud, "This isn't going to hold," and begins to run up hill. Taking out his radio, he quickly gets in touch with Kevin and relays to start moving everyone back up hill. "Things are looking bad down here."

Kevin, not sensing the urgency, yells backward, "Let's R.T.O." meaning reverse tool order. We simply turned around and started hiking back up the mountain thinking Obadi must have tied in with the hotshots.

We hiked for about an hour before someone spotted Obadi running out of the smoke as fast as he could uphill toward us waving his arms telling us to, "Move it." We started walking faster.

As he caught up with us, he stopped for a breath, leaning on his knees. In bits of broken English he blurts out, "Drop gear. Run!" He stands and points back behind him as we all look and see an orange glow growing out of the smoke, making the hairs on the back of your neck tingle. He says again louder, "Run!" Again no one moves and only watches behind Obadi as a single deer jumps through the smoke. It stops momentarily to look at all the yellow stirts, then dashes on up the mountain. It was kind of funny until this low roaring sound builds louder as if a freight train is coming form down in the direction behind the spot the deer was standing. A red glow pushes through the smoke as a bush ignites into flames and a chain reaction starts a wall of flames and climbs the into the branches of the tall pine trees. Reaching up and over the fire line like fingers. Racing up the mountain side toward our positions. Smiles fade as two of the rear firefighters take off running past crewmembers in front of them. Everyone takes off running for his or her own life. The wind can be felt pushing us upward. The faster people are pushing by others and racing up to the logging road, hoping it isn't too far off. Obadi catches up with me grabbing my harness and says," Move it if you want to live boy" as he tears on by.

The last bit of fire-line before reaching the road is so steep that everyone has to crawl up using hands and knees, causing a jam up. Some start trying to traverse off the fire-line making it to the road. Others wait stacked up behind each other for help up the last little bit. Obadi is on top of the road pushing people down

232

and yelling to deploy fire shelters. Embers start flying by us, not falling, but being carried past us. The heat starts to rise. Everyone is yelling, "Move it! MOVE IT! I had just gotten up to the road somehow in the middle of the pack when Obadi pushes me to the ground yelling, "Deploy. Goddammit!" He races back down the fire-line to help the slower crewmembers starting to drift up the fire-line.

The orange glow was all around us now and a loud noise was starting to build like that of a large jet engine thrust. The heat was unbearable. I took one last look around and ducked into my shelter.

The noise got louder and louder and people were screaming, adding to the intensity of the situation. The wind got so strong that it felt as if giant hands were grabbing at my shelter, wind generated force pulling it one way, then another. The heat and noise became unbearable. The natural reaction in my head is telling me to get up and run, but I find myself paralyzed, unable to move. Thoughts of dying sprang up in my head and I quickly replace them with positive sayings like "NO! I'm not dying here". I can't help but scream out for life. At this point, no one can hear me because the noise is like a freight train passing by, in conjunction with a loud jet engine. I can't breathe and my body is hyperventilating for air. I can't help but wiggle around side to side kicking my feet on the ground because of the heat. I pray for every forgiveness and scream, desperately scratching a hole in the ground to find cooler air. Saying over and over again "I am not dying here."

Just about the time I think I can't stand it any longer, it slowly subsides, only to start back up again. It's the same intensity, but this time my body has adjusted a little more to it. It subsides for yet another onslaught of hot air. Finally, the noise begins to fade and I soon recognize the crackling sounds of burning wood. I start to breathe easier. Then, the heat slowly starts to subside. That's when I notice people crying next to me or, it might be my own crying. We stayed put for a long time because some of us are so exhausted we couldn't move. I had gotten so scared my body depleted all energy resources, finding a terrible urge to urinate. I passed out to sleep for a little while. Only to be scared awake by a loud crashing sound to my left then several more off in the distances. Finally dead silence except for an occational crackling of timber burning.

Soon, I came back to life hearing people move around, getting out and walking around, looking and calling out for help. As I crawl out from underneath my fire shelter the first thing I notice is how bare and blackened the landscape is. It doesn't look anything like the green pine and pinon brush that once stood shading the road and hanging over the fire-line. Some people are sitting with their arms out crying in pain. Others are trying to help the best they can. I see were Sara and Hoser had deloyed with a burning snag laying right next to Sara's shelter. She is being helped by Hoser tieing a bandage around her arm. I franticly make my way toward her.

I hear Obadi's voice behind me coming up the road. He finds one of the squad bosses and gives him instructions about getting everyone gathered up. The squad boss says something about a wide turnaround point on up the road a bit. Obadi shakes his head in agreement. Tyron comes up to Obadi and Obadi quickly puts a hand on Tyron's shoulder and holds out his radio. Obadi then bends down to get a breath. With his hands on his knees, I can hear Obadi explaining that he can't get any transmission from this point. He instructs Tyron to run to the highest point of the mountain somewhere on up the road and keep trying until he reaches base camp. "Tell them what's happened and we need help! There may be fatalities! Hey and for God sake watch-out for snags falling, Move man move!" At that point the squad boss turns back around as Obadi continues saying, "That's why I need a body count "Now". Let's go people. Start gathering everyone up and stage at that turnaround place up there." Obadi heads back down the road. He stops and turns toward me saying, "Hey, make sure we are all accounted for Wildman."

When we get to the staging area, the squad boss announces fourteen. Fourteen crewmembers out of the twenty we started with. Everyone is unusually quiet except for the moans from the severely injured. We're all in a state of shock questioning what just happened.

After a long period, Obadi walks back up the road with another crewmember. It's hard to distinguish who is who for the black soot covering everyone. Once Obadi ties in with us he wants to know the count. The squad boss mutters, "Sixteen, counting you two." Obadi ask, "Did we count Tyron? Is he back, yet?" Someone answered, "No!" Obadi thinks out loud, "Okay, that's seventeen. We're missing three unaccounted crewmembers. And that's about right with what I last saw taking off up the mountain. Okay, I am going to need some volunteers to help me start a grid search."

No one moves at first. He continues, "Look, we have three crewmembers still missing out there somewhere in need of our help. Now who is able to help me out and go look for our friends?" Six of us stand up and walk toward Obadi who takes a knee on the sandy road. He starts drawing a picture. "We are here. The fire line goes like this. This is where you all deployed. I last saw some crewmembers taking off in this direction. The mountain ridge runs like this. This logging road snakes around like this. Now, we will start our grid search here and work our way south on this side of the mountain. Their best chance of survival is on this side of the mountain. We will go all the way until we reach the road on the other side. Then we will start back in this direction on the side of the mountain we deployed on. Now, if we find them we might not like what we see. It's important, if they are alive, not to show any weird faces. Tell them everything is going to be al-right. Is that understood? It's very important. Let's line up and move out. And please watch for falling snags. I know I don't have to say that to you all, right?"

236

It was starting to get dark when we began our search. We didn't find anything on the first sweep. However, on our way back, about halfway into the sweep near the top of the ridge, we came upon the first body; fire shelter still in his hand, not even opened. At this point, looking down on the logging road, we could see and hear a parade of vehicles slowly following a dozer up the mountain. Obadi sent one guy down to the road to mark the spot of the find. As we continued a few steps farther, we came upon a helmet. A little further a fire shelter was spotted. Underneath laid Kevin. His eyes were still open and he was still alive. Obadi raced over grabbing his shoulders. Skin slid off, like holding onto a hot, freshly, roasted marshmallow we kids used to cook over a campfire back in the day. Bending down, as close as he could to hear Kevin whisper something Obadi cried out, "Go, get help!" Someone ran down to the road and stopped the parade of lights. Obadi kept saying over and over, "Hang in there old timer! You hang in there!" But, by the time help arrived, Kevin had already faded out. Obadi sat there holding Kevin's head in his lap, rocking back and forth, sobbing.

The rest of us lined back up and continued another ten feet to stumble onto the last victim. The fire shelter was pulled out and flapping by the side of this last crewmember, less than ten feet from the top. Why they didn't stop on the road would be speculated for years to come.

When the investigative team arrived, they loaded all

the crewmembers on a yellow school bus. The rest returned to their respectable engines. The many injuried were taken to the hospital. Not one word was said on the ride back down. We stayed up there on that mountain past midnight. The pueblo wanted a medicine man to come up and release the fallen firefighters' warrior spirit. Once he got up there, he got everyone together and did a prayer on all of us.

A forest supervisor got us all together next to explain that the bus was going to lead us back down to the village. A lot of press was waiting and knowing what we had been through, he thought it best for us not to point fingers, maybe saying something out of context. They had an information officer down there explaining what the press needed to know at this time. He wanted us all to go home to our families. Tomorrow we would have a traumatic stress counseling session. No one said a word.

That's the last I ever saw of Obadi, sitting up there on that mountain rocking back and forth, comforting this fallen warrior as if a child who had lost his dear old dog; his only friend in the world.

It started drizzling rain on the way down the mountain that night, a sad but fitting ending to that experience. For indigenous people, rain marks the renewal of life.

I went to see Red in the Albuquerque St. Joseph Hospital a few days later. She was sitting up watching CNN on TV and seemed to be in a cheerful mood as she blurts out, "Hey you, what's up?" As she turns away to look out the window catching a glimpse of a strange looking little bird out on the landing. It peeks into the window. I wait a moment not believing what I see and slowly mutter, "Has anyone come by to talk with you about the incident?" She looks back at me in surprise saying, "Who?" I continue, "The press?" There is a long pause as we both look back at the window with the strange little bird still looking around and occasionally bathing himself with his head ducking under one wing. Finally she answers, "No, I saw a Forest Service guy talking to some people out in the hallway. Why? What's going on?"

So I proceeded in recounting the events leading up to and after the burnover as I could recall. Then she related the events as she recalled, which was identical to mine, up to the part of the snag falling. She related that the snag had come so close to her that part of her shelter had gotten pinned underneath and Hoser, at one point, got out of his shelter and pulled her into his. I told her that we had to do a search for some of our crew and how Obadi found Kevin. I also had found out that two of our Engines got caught in the burnover as well. She was dumbfounded stating, "Nothing was on the news!" Making me blurt in, "You kidding me Red? Come on you know how this works. Obadi said it himself at the start of that detail, remember? If you ever had to use your shelter in the first place, someone higher up must have really screwed up. That's why they don't want us talking." Red's mouth opens and she shakes her head then points a finger out toward the hallway saying, "So this all didn't happen and it all is suppose to be forgotten? I walked toward the window sill as the strange looking bird gives one quick look around and flys off. I look off into the New Mexico horizon as dark rain clouds can be seen developing off in the distance. I mumble back, "Not Really! Red, hero's die in this business. We can't forget that! We all know the price to pay to get to play with mother nature. I'm no Hero but I'm alive. We have to share this. It's really like what Obadi always use to preach, Never forget ... Good training comes with experience. Lessons learned comes from bad experiences." Red smiles and reaches for my hand as she softly states, "Well, you motor on, I'm counting my blessings and getting out. That was my last fire call."

The official accident investigation report summary read like this:
Buchanan Prescribe Fire
Dated June 28, 1993

Background
Santa Fe National Forest personnel planned the Buchanan Prescribed Fire project over a period of 18 months. The planning was assisted by Forest Service Regional Office specialists in consultation with interested federal and state agencies and included public involvement and several public meetings.

Objectives included reducing buildup of down, woody material that can lead to major wildfires; creating openings in heavy timber to improve wildlife habitat;

regenerating oak brush stands, grass, and forage to improve nutritional value of wildlife browse; and improving timber stands and watershed conditions.

This was a large complex prescribed fire, covering 15,400 acres on Santa Fe National Forest and on Pueblo of Jemez and Pueblo of Zia land. Both Pueblos cooperated with the Forest Service in burning portions of their land to meet Pueblo resource objectives and to take advantage of topography and roads. Project planning was in order and well documented.
Crews ignited the fire by hand and from helicopters using several methods.

Some ground crews used "drip torches" to ignite fires. Drip torches contain a diesel-gasoline mix dripped from hand-held torches to ignite fires.

Other crews used terra-torches. These are containers mounted on vehicles that pump and ignite a jellied gasoline mixture from a hand-held wand. They are used along roads or where there is vehicle access.

Inaccessible portions of the fire were ignited form helicopters with "helitorches" and "ping pong ball machines." A helitorch is a large container suspended beneath a helicopter that drops jellied gasoline. A "ping pong ball machine" is a device that injects ethylene glycol into plastic spheres filled with potassium permanganate powder that ignite after they reach the ground.

The Buchanan Prescribed Fire was conducted from April 20-23. The project proceeded without incident until Thursday, April 22, at 3:40 p.m.

Events of Thursday, April 23 1993.

Crews with drip torches began igniting fires at 10:30 a.m. at the junction of Pajarito Peak road and Penasco Canyon. Terra-torch operations began at 11:30 a.m. in the bottom of Penaso Canyon. A change in wind direction caused the terra-torch crew to stop firing at 11:45 a.m. At 12:15 p.m., the wind direction was once again favorable and the terra-torch crew began firing operations along the east side of the road in Penasco Canyon. The terra-torch ran out of fuel at 1:30 p.m. and the crew began returning to Pajarito Peak Road.

A back-fire that crews from Engine 3 and 5 had started to protect Archaeological Site 2795 was visible from Pajarito Peak Road at 1:30 p.m. The terra-torch crew arrived at this fire at 2:00 p.m. The fire was about two acres and very active.

Helicopter 300 dropped ping pong balls east of Pajarito Peak Road in a series of three north-south runs of approximately ¼ mile each at 2:45 p.m. The south end of each run was even with Site 1. This drop was made to help strengthen the fire line below Pajarito Peak Road. Crews igniting fires by hand from the road had not made much progress because of sparse ground fuels. Following these three runs, Helicopter 300 dropped ping pong balls at 3:00 p.m.

in one run approximately 100-150 feet below the road from Site 1 to Site 3.

At 3:15 p.m., a single pinon tree below Site 1 ignited, throwing sparks onto the slope above the road. About 10-15 spot fires mostly 2-3 inches in diameter started, but were controlled by the Engine 9 crew and Jemez crew. The largest spot fire grew to three feet in diameter before it was controlled.

Because there was no great concern about the Jemez crew's or Engine 9 crew's ability to locate and control spots. Engine 5 was moved to Site 2 at 3:15 p.m. at this time, there was little wind but the smoke was very thick. Two squads from the Jemez crew were on the slope above Pajarito Peak Road looking for and suppressing spot fires.

A "major wind event" was reported at 3:38 p.m. at Site 1. At 3:40 p.m., the wind increased to 40-45 miles per hour and shifted form west to southwest, causing the ground fire in the area below the road at Site 3 to ignite the tops of the trees and make a short run east. This fire then crossed the road at Site 4 and moved at about a 45-degree angle northeast across the south-facing slope.

At the time, 16 crew members were threatened or trapped by the fire. Four people at Site 2 successfully used three fire shelters. Ten people chose to not use their fire shelters and escaped the flame front by getting to the road north of Site 1 or behind Engine 9 at Site 1. One man at Site 2 had difficulty opening his shelter and chose to move down below the road to an area already burned. One person above Pajarito Peak Road, did not escape the flame front.

Because of the wind's sudden shift and increased speed, he had virtually no warning. As he ran uphill toward a ridge line, he tried to open and enter his fire shelter just before the flame front reached him, but could not. The fire had spread too quickly up the steep slope for him to outrun the flame front.

Analysis of physical evidence at the fatality site showed that the fire burned at temperatures from 1,500-2,000 degrees Fahrenheit, which is not survivable even in a fire shelter, unless used in a large clearing. At these temperatures, protective fire clothing fails in 10-16 seconds and a fire shelter in about 25 seconds.

Between 3:40 p.m. and 3:50 p.m., several flame fronts passed over the people near Engines 5 and 9. Three men near Engine 5 were able to successfully open their fire shelters on the road about 100 feet east of Engine 5 and enter them.

At 3:45 p.m., the men in fire shelters emerged. Carrying their shelters they moved toward Engine 5.

At 3:46 p.m., another fire front approached from the southwest. They re-entered their shelters about 20-30 feet in front of Engine 5.

The wind slowed at 3:48 p.m. and the men remained

in their fire shelters until the smoke cleared, then emerged at 4:07 p.m.

When a roll call of all personnel in the area was completed at 5:00 p.m., it was determined that four were missing and a grid search began. The bodies were located at 5:53 p.m.

Reading this, it still makes me mad…

Retirement Party

Back at the retirement party, John-John was clenching the podium tight with both hands.
He continues his speech. *"I say this for all of you; Wildland firefighting is a culture of hardship (the crowd boos), adventure (the group cheers), close friendships (someone yells out,"Can I have your boots?"), and commitment (Someone else hollers "What else can we do?"). Many young firefighters believe that a hard day's work for a fair day's pay describes the average day in wildland firefighting. (HA!) Admittedly, there are debates, disagreements, and major issues within this community (some say dysfunctional). This culture, described by the firefighters respects experience over rank, values an aggressive attitude in the face of hardship, enjoys stories of conquest and danger, and is proud of how different the life of a wildland firefighter is from nearly everyone else's (the group cheers "Here, Here!"). My career has cultivated that culture, starting out at the bottom as a crewmember on a*

*typical squad of seasonal wildland firefighters
working my way up through the ranks to managing
you yahoos. It is a culture that is described as both
broad and deep. As such, each individual member
carries his or her own mental photo album of what
that culture is. It includes the attitudes and beliefs
of us all. We are all from different nationalities and
areas of expertise, coming together to battle a force
of nature. How foolish of man to think he has
control over this violent force. The true flurry of the
beast will engrain itself wholeheartedly into the lives
and minds of all that dare to cross its path, proving
over and over again how vulnerable the human
spirit really is. Fire creates profound respect from
all natural elements and driving forces around us.
Appreciate this day, today, everyday, as if it would
be the last. I can't help but to look around at all
these young faces and remember the family and
friends that got me here. I have promised to share
that always, and never forget how it all began."*

He stops speaking and looks directly over at the
elderly lady whom he married 35 years ago. She
lowers her head, wiping tears from her face.

Wiping the tears off his face he looks up saying,
"Now's it's your turn young bloods. I would like to
leave you all something to think about." He reaches
into his back pants pocket and pulls out a piece of
folded paper. At this time he wipes his eyes and
clears his throat before continuing the speech. It's a
poem by a good friend and fellow fire fighter of
mine. It's called "IN MEMORY":

As I visited the firefighters memorial,
In a trance, I wondered about,
A tear comes to my eye.
I swear at the true act of heroism, "The ones who
have fallen, swept up by time."
When a firefighter duels with the flames of a raging
inferno,
To save your way of life, your home, your land, your
dreams, the ones you love.
He gives all, to save his brother, in war,
Like a Sacrificial Dove.

Hero's by choice and forgotten in time.
They battled the elements of nature.
They battled the fear of mankind.
Their prayer God's intervention to even the score

We will miss them, I know for I do,
They were and are my friends and I will join them
some day.
Their numbers are many they answered their last fire
call, and now have gone on.
Like prayers fading with the smoke.

What can you do in return?
Be careful with nature, admire her beauty, and show
respect for her power.

And in memory visit my bro's memorials.
For they have left their loved ones behind, and faced
their fears answering the final fire call.
Signed-The Fire Poet

Just as he finishes a commotion erupts off stage to the right as one of the older gentlemen comes up to John-John and whispers something into his ear.

John-John doesn't lose a beat as he continues, "Funny thing is this would be my luck and fitting. All you fire dogs out there have a fire call right now. So this is it here for me. It's been a hoot. You all go and be safe out there. Don't be Hero's!" He looks out over the crowd as all the firefighters don yellow shirt, kissing thier love-one's and start to move out. John-John shakes his head and just walks back to his seat to join his wife-Red. Who is still seated in her chair as he reaches for her hand, she smile and says, "It's fitting... Let's go home Wildman..."

However as they turn to follow everyone out, something in the very back catches his eye. He puts on his glasses to get a better look, saying, "Ah it's....." All of the sudden he shakes his head as if to clear a thought. He looks again toward the back. Sara starts to grab for him thinking, oh my, he is going to faint.

Sitting out by the road on a new fully dressed-out Harley Davidson Fat-boy motorbike is this longhaired Indian dude wearing dark rim sunglasses with a white shirt under a black leather jacket ,well worn blue jeans and dusty cowboy boots. His arms are folded as he listens to the speech.

John-John stays glued to the stranger and continues

saying, "Why... Why that old Dawg..." People stop and turn back looking at John-John and start to question what could be going on.

The stranger slowly gets off his motorbike and starts to make his way up through the crowd. John-John meets him halfway wraps a big bear hug around the stranger. He turns to face everyone that is left. Shakes his head, and smiles saying "Obadi, you ole Dawg, it is damn good too see you."

Conclusion

This story would not be complete with an ending of two old childhood buddies riding off into the sunset on their thundering motorbikes. A couple months after my retirement party, my wife, Sara, and I decided to move our family back to North Carolina and invest our life savings into taking over my parents' old gift shop. It took a lot of persuading, but I also got my best childhood friend to go in partners with me. Obadi and I now have all the free time in this world to ride around to different states, hitting various blues concerts and cultural gatherings.

Who knows? If you ever end up on a big complex fire incident somewhere out west, you still may be fortunate enough to actually run across a story of this longhaired Native American firefighter. Or, if you are fortunate enough to see him, ask him to tell you a story. He probably has many to share.

On Obadi's fiftieth birthday I was stumped on what to get him as a repayment and gesture for being a friend through all these difficult seasons. My twelve-year-old son recommended a puppy, not just any old mutt, but a fuzzy black mutt with a white speck running between his eyes.

I have to tell you this; as my wife along with my son and I packed up the food that we had prepared to take to the feast that follows most reservation family birthday celebrations. We all couldn't wait to get rid of this devilish beast of a pup. It had chewed every shoe and piece of leather in our house. As we enter the reservation boundaries I couldn't help but stare in awe at the beauty surrounding this place. The rivers and streams looked invitingly cool and fresh as the tall green trees shaded the landscape blocking out the hot humid August heat of the south. Driving around curves and more curves, up and down long steep mountains, simply got this pup sick. My wife was about to come unglued because of the mess the pup put on her black leather car seats. My own son had his head sticking out the back window trying not to be sick himself. That pup! It is said around these parts that the dog acts like the master that feeds it. This pup hadn't even met his master yet but you could tell he already acted like his master to be. Just plain naughty!

Obadi's birthday dawned a bright, sunny morning, the perfect setting for the delivery of his new pup. The pup was quickly named, "Hey Dawg or damn dog." At any rate it was like seeing this old man revisit his childhood days. Obadi simply couldn't hold back all the emotions that flooded him as he sat on the living-room carpet weeping rivers of tears, hugging the pup as it jumped around in his lap, licking his face. My family didn't really know what to say, but my wife and I understood. We sat in silence, patiently watching this long awaited event unfold. Later on, he would thank my son, saying it was the best gift anyone could have offered him.

Of course, now there's a compartment on the side of Obadi's bike where "Hey Dog" rides. It even has Obadi out running the trails in the Great Smokey Mountains again. After all, I think that was my greatest gift, being able to finally show this one lost Native soul a way home, to family. Now, maybe he will never have to ride another bus, watching his freedom pass by, wondering if he will ever have a place to call "home".

After the feast of a dinner Obadi and his sons showed us around their native home. It sat perched along side this beautiful mountain side. On the back patio one could see for miles and miles of green rolling mountains. Coming back into the Living room you had to step down some rock steps onto a shiny oak floor covered with a rug designed with southwestern pueblo patterns. To one corner was a rock fire place covered with different types of Indian pottery and a framed mirror on top. The couches where draped with several beautiful wool Pendleton blankets which sat in the middle of the floor facing the fire place. Four huge glass windows looked out onto the patio and the mountains. Lining the interior walls at the back where two-glass displays lit full of pictures and trophies. It looked like a museum more than a reservation home, and "No" Cherokees don't live in teepees.

I had to stop and look at the pictures as Obadi's son walks back to where I am and says, "He has a story for each one." I reply back "I bet he does," leaving him to usher the rest of my family up stairs as I go back out side where Obadi is standing looking out over the mountains. We both just stand there taking in the beautiful scenery. It starts to rain. Obadi holds out his arms and looks up into the partly cloudy sky and in a low tone says "I use to hate this. You Know? The old Cherokees say water is a symbolism of cleansing. The waters of the river ("Long Man") were always believed to be sacred to the Cherokee and believe that the water is a sacred messenger and commonly used for purification and other ceremonies.

My wife told me of the days she remembered when her father use to take her to the mountain stream in back of their house just before dawn and splash cold mountain water over her head seven times and praying for her health and safety. I also heard this from my grandma, with a lot of prayer, and persistence's from my other family members, I eventually gave in to follow the Red-Road of sobriety. We also sat up a meeting with a traditional medicine man. I was thinking what the hell, I might as well get back to culture and see if there was true healing to this cleansing ceremony.

The old Cherokee medicine man started out talking about life. "I hear a fight is going on inside you-son," he said to me. "It is a terrible fight and it is between two wolves. One is evil - he is anger, envy, sorrow, regret, greed, arrogance, self-pity, guilt, resentment, inferiority, lies, false pride, superiority, and ego. The other is good - he is joy, peace, love, hope, serenity, humility, kindness, benevolence, empathy, generosity, truth, compassion, and faith. This same fight is going on inside every other person, too." This made Obadi thinks for a minute and then asked the medicine man, "Which wolf will win?" As the old Cherokee medicine man gets up and walks outside he simply replied, "The one you feed, come." We talked more about what to expect if I was to continue this "going to water," as it is called. He said it is performed on a great variety of occasions, such as at each new moon, before eating the new food at the green corn dance, before the medicine dance and other ceremonial dances before and after the ball play, in connection with the prayers for long life, to counteract the effects of bad dreams or the evil spells of an enemy, and as a part of the regular treatment in various diseases. The ceremony generally is performed just at daybreak. The bather usually dips completely under the water four or seven times, but in some cases it is sufficient to pour the water from the hand upon the head and breast. The latter part of autumn is deemed the most suitable season of the year for this ceremony, as the leaves which then cover the surface of the stream are supposed to impart their medicinal virtues to the water.

That would only be one part of this ceremony. Water and religion are central to the spirituality of all Native Americans and their beliefs. However, the water was not always the type that is flowing or contained in lakes. One ritual practiced by all tribes was the Sweat Lodge ritual which caused water to leave the human body via perspiration and was a cleansing and detoxifying process.

We started with an offering of tobacco. In turn he directed me to a fast for several days. After that I was put into a hot sweat lodge where we sang traditional songs and prayers while beating on the drum. Next, I was washed in cold water from the river then finally fed a huge feast. At the feast all my loved ones gathered and hosted a traditional Cherokee Stomp dance.

Has it worked? All I can say is, I know my culture. I love my family and choose to walk a different road. I take it one day at a time and life is good to me. I choose to keep myself in balance with the physical and the spiritual elements of this world. I pray every morning facing the east like my forefathers. I know now what I did not know back then and that's the difference. All warrior's need a cleansing, a change of heart. Letting go. You know old buddy, in all my tragedies from childhood to man I have been told we always go through three phrases of healing. First is denial, the part where we can't believe what just happened. Second, blame or guilt and finally release. I know a lot of my bro's have a hard time with this last part because I sure did. But you know old friend my only true regret was thinking I could let go of family and friends. Trying to take on the burden of the world on my own. If it wasn't for friends and family like you, people like me would never find peace and happiness. Thanks bro!

With that Obadi lets out a loud Cherokee war call. One that is usually heard at all the annual Fall Festival stick ball games. I couldn't help but do the challenging answer-call. A moment after that a flash of lightning laminates the dark clouds as a rumbling resonates down through the valley. Standing there soaked to the bone we first look at each other then we both laughed and run back in the house to be with our families.

We all have some wonderful stories to share. Unfortunately, most die off with the person who lived it. My own Indian culture has lost a lot of our past knowledge of this land because of this so-called improved, dominating society we now have to live in. The old ways of passing on our oral history often falls onto young deaf ears eager to forget the past for the desire to fit into the present. I could not let this happen here.

An old Ogallala Sioux named Black Elk Speaks sums this up in his autobiography that he dictated in 1931. *"You have noticed that everything an Indian does is in a circle, and that is because the Power of the Universe always works in circles, and everything tries to be round. In the old days when we were a strong and happy people, all our power came to us from the sacred hoop of the nation, and so as long as the hoop was unbroken, the people flourished. The flowering tree was the living center of the hoop, and the circle of the four quarters nourished it. The east gave peace and light, the south gave warmth, the west gave rain, and the north with its cold and mighty wind gave strength and endurance. This knowledge came to us from the outer world with our religion. Everything the Power of the World does is done in a circle. The sky is round and I have heard that the earth is round like a ball and so are all the stars. The wind, in its greatest power, whirls. Birds make their nests in circles, for theirs is the same religion as ours. The sun comes forth and goes down again in a circle. The moon does the same, and both are round. Even the seasons form a great circle in their changing and always come back again to where they were. The life of man is a circle from childhood to childhood and so it is in everything where power moves. Our teepees were round like the nests of birds and these were always set in a circle, the nation's hoop a nest of many nests where the Great Spirit meant for us to raise our families."*

Obadi has always been a big part of my family, giving me direction, purpose and always willing to be like a big brother that I never had. Without him, I would have never had the courage to venture past my own protected world. Nor would I have been fortunate enough to see the great beauty that this land we live in has to offer or learn the culture of my own people. I might not have met this amazing wife who bore our children, without living through the extension of my childhood friend. I owe him this much at least. And true to his humble nature, he would never think to ask anything other than to have this story told. Chief Seattle sums it up nicely by stating *"When the last red man shall have become a myth among the white men, when your children's children think themselves alone in the field, upon the highway or in the silence of the pathless woods, they will not be alone. In all the earth there is no place dedicated to solitude. At night when the streets of your cities are silent, they will throng with the returning hosts that once filled them and still love this beautiful land..."*

This is our story.
The end?
Why, it's only beginning.
Like the changing of seasons.

In Cherokee we say "dv-na-da-go-nv-i"

Meaning "til we meet again"

"In dedication to all the Native Americans Wildland Firefigthers whose fate ended undocumented protecting one of our nations natural resources. May we never forget their voices." Stephan Ray Swimmer